Mother Tongue or Second Language?

On the Teaching of Reading in Multilingual Societies

Dina Feitelson, Editor
University of Haifa
Haifa, Israel

Includes selected papers from the
Sixth IRA World Congress on Reading
Singapore
August 17-19, 1976

International Reading Association
800 Barksdale Road
Newark, Delaware   United States of America

Copyright 1979 by the
International Reading Association, Inc.

Library of Congress Cataloging in Publication Data
World Congress on Reading, 6th, Singapore, 1976.
     Mother tongue or second language? On the Teaching of
Reading in Multilingual Societies
     "Includes selected papers from the Sixth IRA World
Congress on Reading, Singapore, August 17-19, 1976."
     Includes bibliographies.
     1. Reading—Congresses. I. Feitelson, Dina.
II. International Reading Association. III. Title.
LB1049.95.W67 1976a   428'.4   78-16025
ISBN 0-87207-426-9

Contents

iii

Acknowledgements

Except for one, all of the papers in this volume were prepared for the Sixth World Congress on Reading held by the International Reading Association in Singapore in August 1976. The chapter by Fellman was written especially for this volume. As editor, I am grateful to all of these contributors.

I am especially grateful to Connie McCullough, who appointed me Program Chairperson for the Singapore Congress. In addition, I wish to thank the members of the IRA Publications Committee for their approval of this volume for publication and their invitation to me to serve as editor. I also thank Lloyd Kline, Faye Branca, and Romayne McElhaney for their advice and help throughout the development of this volume, especially for their good offices in rendering in readable English the papers of those of us for whom English is not a native language.

DF

Foreword

Bilingual people must have existed even in very olden times, but the problem of "mother tongue or second language" in teaching reading did not seem to appear in the days when the number of bilingual people was small and when reading was an activity of only the so-called elite. As the number of bilingual people increased, and as society required more literate people for its functions, this problem started to attract the interest of some reading professionals, mainly in the major English-speaking countries.

At present, there are a great many bilingual people around the world. In addition, reading has become very essential to everyone's life in modern society. No one doubts, regardless of the complicating factors, that all people have the right to read and that teachers are responsible for their pupils' becoming literate.

It was quite natural for the Sixth World Congress on Reading, which was held in Singapore in 1976, to have scholars from many different countries reporting on the problem of bilingualism in their own countries. Now is the time to study this phenomenon, not only for English-speaking people, but also for people for whom English is neither the first nor the second language.

There are quite a variety of cases of bilingualism in relation to teaching children to read, varying according to the combination of languages in the child's immediate environment. Take a look at some cases which can be imagined in a family. The most typical might be the family in which the native tongue of both the father and the mother is language A. The child, however, might speak language A and also language B, the language used in society and taught at school. This happens to immigrant families in many countries. Another possible combination: language A is used by the father and the mother but language B is spoken by the child, even though language A is taught in school. Such is the case when a Japanese businessman and his wife return with their child from a foreign country where they have lived for a long time and where the child was born. When the parents' native languages are different from each other, things are even more complicated and many more combinations become possible.

Sometimes, we simply attribute educational problems involved in any of these combinations to bilingualism in general, but the precise nature of the problem differs from one combination to another and each needs to be treated differently. To begin with, we must know what kind of bilingual problem exists, where and how widespread it is.

The International Reading Association has a history of more than twenty years. It seems that only recently, however, has the Association grown into its label, "international." It should be noted that the "railroad" carrying the Association to true internationalism could never have been laid without the efforts of more than a few scholars whose mother language is not English. Dina Feitelson is one of those scholars.

This volume, edited by Dr. Feitelson, depicts what is going on in the teaching of reading in multilingual societies, and where. It seems to me that the tracks are now down and this book is the first train to depart for our "international" destination on the brand new line. Not only people in the educational field but also people from other academic disciplines, as well as such people as diplomats, business-men, and parents will be on board once they realize that we all live in one rapidly changing small world.

TAKAHIKO SAKAMOTOA
Director, Department of Reading
Noma Institute of Educational Research
Tokyo, Japan

Introduction

Dina Feitelson

MULTILINGUALISM AND READING: A REAPPRAISAL*

The complex area of providing suitable educational experiences for American children in whose homes standard English is not the main medium of communication has, in recent years, become a focus of widespread interest and concern (*3, 7, 11, 12*), a concern which led to federal funding of bilingual education programs. Undoubtedly, one of the reasons for this development was the tendency to associate poor school performance, and especially difficulties in reading of minority group children, with the fact that the language of instruction in school differed from that used in homes and neighborhoods. Providing initial reading experiences in a familiar idiom would, it was argued, lead to greater success in the acquisition of reading as well as improve self-image and attitude toward the home community. Most of the literature available to the American professional, in this fast developing field, is of relatively recent origin and deals with the problems of multilingualism within the context of minority groups living in a predominantly unilingual culture. In these circumstances, issues of bilingualism per se were sometimes confounded with problems of social status, migration, and/or learning problems. Also, the scholars involved were most often members of a majority language group, even when they had acquired proficiency in a second or third language for professional or other purposes.

---

*The author is indebted to A. D. Cohen for helpful discussions and access to recent literature in the preparation of this chapter.

It is the aim of the present volume to make a modest beginning toward a considerable broadening of the perspectives in which problems of bilingual or, as we prefer to call it in the present context, multilingual education are considered.

The complex interacting forces, so often part and parcel of a naturalistic multilingual situation, do not lend themselves well to controlled reproducible experimentation so that there is scant hope for rigorous, encompassing research results within the near future. Instead, this volume provides a series of vivid vignettes of the problems, the conflicting tendencies, and the dynamics of reaching educational decisions in present day multilingual societies. In every case, the authors are personally involved in the processes they describe. Often they are members of the educational establishment on the scene, decision-makers or implementers rather than observers from outside (be they ever so benign and well intentioned). Further, the authors and the editor live in predominantly multilingual societies, so that for them constant switching from medium to medium is a matter of natural daily norm, scarcely even noticed or thought of consciously. In writing their contributions, all but two of the contributors had to use a language acquired in school—one which, in several cases, was not even their second language but rather a third or fourth. It is hoped that their descriptions will contribute to a greater appreciation of the fact that, in many present day nations, multilingualism is a way of life and that there are many common elements in multilingual situations.

It may well be that in recent years, when the majority of educational resources and research efforts were located in countries predominantly unilingual, not enough attention was paid to the effects of multilingualism or to the characteristics of individuals who are habitual users of more than one language. It would be well to remember that the very notion of a common national language originated fairly recently within the framework of the nineteenth century Revolutionary period. According to Lewis (8), "Romanticism, nationalism, and the rise of modern philology are contemporaneous and associated features." Till then, and all through Western history, multilingualism was viewed favorably as an attribute of the privileged classes or of the learned.

Lewis (8) documents in detail the long history of bilingualism, and shows that proficiency in second and sometimes third languages was a widespread phenomenon all the way back to antiquity. In more recent times, acquiring an education was nearly synonymous with a study of classic languages and classic texts in the original, while university learning was completely in Latin. In secondary education, extensive study of classic languages persisted to the present century. Throughout this period, the study of classic languages was also considered an important tool for shaping and exercising young minds (5). Put into present day terminology, this would mean that it was essentially considered as a way of furthering cognitive development.

It was only within the more recent past that the question arose of a possible negative effect of bilingualism on level of cognitive functioning. When it did, it was invariably within the context of unsatisfactory school performance of minority group children within unilingual majority school systems. Most often the situation was considerably compounded by social class effects or recent migration, such as when the children concerned were from Welsh mining villages or American Indian reservations or their families had migrated from the West Indies, Puerto Rico, or Mexico.

Reexaminations of early studies, which purported to document negative effects of bilingualism on school performance and achievement on intelligence tests, have shown that most of the studies were not well controlled for social class, motivational factors, or extent and circumstances of the use of the two languages (10). New research evidence (1, 2, 9) does, in fact, support earlier intuitive assertions about the beneficial influence of bilingualism per se. Not only is there no evidence that bilingualism causes an impairment of cognitive functioning, but quite the contrary. When subjects were carefully matched on relevant variables, bilinguals demonstrated superior abilities on certain abstract skills so that researchers tended to conclude that they were freed from the "tyranny of words"; showed a greater degree of "mental flexibility"; and were aware at an earlier age that symbolic systems were arbitrary and could be manipulated at will.

Further, there is a growing tendency to attribute to motivational factors and the direct effects of particular learning environments the apparent discrepancy between favorable reports on the results of bilingual education and the many accounts of difficulty experienced by minority children. Ferguson, Houghton, and Wells (6) mention in this context dialect speaking Schwabisch children who acquire school German without apparent difficulty as both they and their community regard this as a natural part of their school experience in contrast to many American Black children who have trouble with standard

American School English, not because they lack innate ability, but because "neither they nor the community expect them to acquire the school register, and they do not."

There is little doubt that one of the origins of the interest in bilingual education and the upsurge in bilingual education programs was the often voiced assertion that reading should be taught in the vernacular. In the historic Unesco conference, resulting in the monograph *The Use of Vernacular Languages in Education* (1953), the assembled experts established as axiomatic that the best medium for teaching literacy was in the mother tongue of the pupil.

It is, therefore, of special interest that recent, well controlled studies (which were a direct result of the interest in bilingual education) seem to prove that under certain conditions it is immaterial whether reading is introduced initially in the first language or in the second, provided certain ground rules are observed (*3, 4*).

The implications of these results could be far reaching indeed, as they could reverse the trend for an extended period of oral training which was so long accepted as indispensible in foreign language learning. In fact, it may well be that the generally poor results of formal foreign language programs for young children reported in the survey by Stern and Weinrib (*13*), in contrast to the relative success of such programs at a later age, could be partly due to the fact that the first relied mainly on audiolingual methods, while at a later age educators did not hesitate to also make use of written language in teaching the new medium.

There seems urgent need for serious research work and sharing of information among educational experts directly active in bilingual and multilingual education in naturalistic settings, and a clear realization of the many ways in which such situations differ from the teaching of a second language to students firmly entrenched in a unilingual environment. Such work, it is hoped, could also provide new evidence about the role of reading in facilitating language development in the two, three, or more languages a child will be acquiring in a multilingual society, rather than make the fact of multilingualism a scapegoat for unsatisfactory performance in reading.

References

1. Balkan, L. Les Effects des Bilingualisme Francaise-Anglaise sur les Aptitudes Intellectuelles. Bruxelles: Aimav, 1970.
2. Ben-Zeev, S. "The Influence of Bilingualism on Problems of Development and Cognitive Strategy," unpublished doctoral dissertation, University of Chicago, 1972.

3. Cohen, A. D. *A Sociolinguistic Approach to Bilingual Education.* Rowley, Massachusetts: Newbury House, 1975.
4. Cohen, A. D., and L. M. Laosa. "Second Language Instruction: Some Research Considerations," *Curriculum Studies,* 8 (1976), 149-165.
5. Cubberly, E. P. *The History of Education.* Boston: Houghton Mifflin, 1920.
6. Ferguson, C. A., C. Houghton, and M. Y. Wells. "Bilingual Education: An International Perspectives," in B. Spolsky and R. L. Cooper (Eds.), *Frontiers of Bilingual Education.* Rowley, Massachusetts: Newbury House, 1977.
7. Fishman, J. A. *Bilingual Education: An International Sociological Perspective.* Rowley, Massachusetts: Newbury House, 1976.
8. Lewis, E. G. "Bilingualism and Bilingual Education: The Ancient World to the Renaissance," in B. Spolsky and R. L. Cooper (Eds.), *Frontiers of Bilingual Education.* Rowley, Massachusetts: Newbury House, 1977.
9. Peal, E., and W. W. Lambert. "The Relation of Bilingualism to Intelligence," *Psychological Monographs,* 76 (1962).
10. Segalowitz, N. "Psychological Perspectives on Bilingual Education," in B. Spolsky and R. L. Cooper (Eds.), *Frontiers of Bilingual Education.* Rowley, Massachusetts: Newbury House, 1977.
11. Simoes, A. (Ed.). *The Bilingual Child.* New York: Academic Press, 1976.
12. Spolsky, B., and R. L. Cooper (Eds.). *Frontiers of Bilingual Education.* Rowley, Massachusetts: Newbury House, 1977.
13. Stern, H. H., and S. Weinrib. "Foreign Languages for Younger Children: Trends and Assessments," *Language Teaching and Linguistics: Abstracts,* 10 (1977), 5-25.

PART ONE

The opening chapter by Gonzalez and the two following it vividly and forcefully portray a situation familiar to members of the societies discussed in this volume. Gonzalez depicts a newly created nation, recently liberated from foreign rule, in the process of forging its national identity to serve as a unifying framework for its often divergent peoples. In these circumstances, a common national language becomes an indispensable tool and a decision is made to adopt or develop one, despite the tremendous practical difficulties of such a course which, to the uninvolved outsider, could well seem insurmountable.

Bear in mind that, in these conditions, the issues being faced and the decisions being made are first and foremost social and political and not ones of educational expediency. A facilitating factor in making such far-reaching decisions, and in accepting with apparent equanimity the fact that they most often mean that every person in the new society will have to be conversant in at least two (and sometimes more) languages, may be found in the recent colonial past of those concerned. After all, had not the preceding period of foreign domination shown that people were well able to function efficiently in a language not their own? In the present case, for instance, English was the medium of instruction in the Philippines for less than forty years. Yet, according to Gonzalez, the students of the day established full command, and proficiency seems to have been considered entirely successful.

The chapters by Boey and Sadtono are further fascinating examples of the rationale accompanying the repudiation of languages reminiscent of a colonial past, be they ever so functional and widely spoken. These feelings seem so strong that the process seems to recur invariably, even in those cases in which the former language has to be retained at least partially for an interim period as medium of higher instruction or for international contacts. Thus, it was only after twenty-nine years of independence that Israel reinstated English as a Eurpoean language in passports, after English had been immediately ousted in favour of French when Israel gained independence from British Mandatory rule.

Interestingly enough, a common feature of the transfer to a new national language mentioned by the present authors but also reported in other countries, is a lowering in the level of performance of the international language formerly deemed satisfactory. It is often impossible to judge whether these assertions would be sustained by objective evidence, as they may perhaps be due to the fact that in colonial times, education was often less widely accessible, so that former attainments were only those of a smaller and possibly more select group than the one studying at present. Also, in colonial times, the foreign language was probably more functional and persons were exposed to it more frequently than after independence. This, too, would result in a higher level of motivation as well as more opportunity to practice.

Curriculum Development and Evaluation in Two Languages

Esperanza A. Gonzalez
Bureau of Secondary Education
Manila, Philippines

Planning the learning experiences of the young in an age of acceptedly exponential rate of curriculum obsolescence is a hazardous exercise. For education must meet the incredibly heightened demands of the changing society even as it serves in the stabilization of the values of that society. Experience, theory, and research, notwithstanding, curriculum planning is at best an act of great faith and hope. Its end product becomes tangible only years hence and after a multiplicity of variables have played on its implementation.

This is nowhere more profoundly felt than in a country that is developing, still bearing the vestiges of a colonial past but eager to assert its new independence and its identity. The society would generally have, among other elements in its culture, a colonial language functioning with the native language/languages in an environment where native values, traditions, and mores would have given way to or made accommodations for the cultural influences of the colonizing power. What must the young learn in schools to be able to perform creditably in such a society? How can it be known that children's education has equipped them to live efficiently and effectively as individuals and as members of this society? Specifically, how is the reading program built in such a context? How is it evaluated?

The Philippines is one such society. Comprising over 7,000 islands, its population (currently 44 million) was long separated, not only by waters but by high and rugged mountain ranges. This contributed to the linguistic and cultural diversities of the eight major language groups as well as the over one hundred minor language speakers in the country.

History, also, has been an important factor in the development of the multilingual-multicultural nation. The effects of Spanish and, subsequently, American occupation of the country are discernible in the names of most Filipinos; in the Spanish and American words that have found their way into the native languages; and in the great many Spanish and American influences on the customs, beliefs, and institutions of the people.

The hallmarks of more than three centuries of Spanish governance of the Filipinos are the churches and the few old Spanish speaking families, remnants of an elite group who were able to avail themselves of the exclusive educational privileges of the period. While the church was for everyone, education was for only a few. Hence, while everyone memorized and recited prayers by rote in Spanish, only the privileged, educated group really communicated in the language.

In contrast, the educational system established by the Americans in 1900 was delivered to the people en masse. This was truly an experiment in democracy and in national unification through language. The diverse language groups of the nation soon were communicating in English which, for expediency, was adopted as the medium of instruction in all the schools. The reading materials were books brought over from the United States. In a few years, the Filipino child was singing American songs, talking of Abraham Lincoln and George Washington, and feeling proud of his democratic way of life. Until 1937, when nationalist president of the Philippine Commonwealth Manuel L. Quezon mandated the teaching of a national language, the sole language in the schools was English. It was also the language of the courts, of business, and of government.

The introduction of Pilipino, the national language, in the schools started a language revolution. Significantly, a great number of Filipinos deplored this as the cause of the deterioration of the Filipino's command of English. On the other hand, those who believed that the Filipino was miseducated because he was being educated in a foreign language (2) considered this a milestone in the renewal of Filipino nationalism. It was no longer punishable (as it used to be) in the schools to speak in Pilipino instead of in English. In a few more years, and after some successful experiments in the use of the vernacular as the medium for learning in the lower grades, other native languages were introduced in the schools. The Filipino child started to learn in his native language during his first two years in school, shifting to English as one of his school subjects in Grade Three, simultaneously learning Pilipino as well.

A great many questions were raised as to the logic and validity of the language teaching situation in the schools. Complaints on the Filipino's inadequacy in both English and Pilipino were raised and repeatedly directed at the policy makers. Experimental efforts were initiated toward the use of Pilipino as the medium of instruction, instead of the vernacular, in the early years of school. However, several language groups argued against this as making the Filipino study two foreign languages and learn subject matter in them at the same time. The reality that Pilipino has fast become the language of radio, television, movies, billboards, street signs, and other printed media seems to have been lost in this argument. Also, the fact that the 1973 Constitution of the Philippines provided for the use of both English and Pilipino as official languages of the nation was not considered by these groups.

In the wake of such confusion, studies and hearings were conducted by the National Board of Education on the basis of which a policy of bilingual education was issued by the Secretary of Education and Culture on March 16, 1973. Subsequently, guidelines (4) were issued on June 19, 1974. These guidelines provided that as soon as the Filipino child entered school, he would learn science and mathematics in English along with English as a language; social studies, practical arts, physical education, and health would be learned in Pilipino, with Pilipino as a subject, if the student was not a speaker of Tagalog (Pilipino). This language dichotomy of the school subjects continues in the secondary school. The aim is for the Filipino to be competent in both English and Pilipino and to be able to take his examinations in either or both languages by 1981.

The present day educated Filipino, therefore, is generally a multilingual—except the Tagalog (Pilipino) speaker. He has a vernacular, the language of his home and family; the national language (Pilipino), a language that he learns in school and that identifies him as a Filipino; and English, the language in which he has been educated so far, and which serves as his link to the bigger world of knowledge and people. His ways and behavior manifest the varied colors of his culture, a mark of most modern societies. Through newspapers, radio,

TV, billboards, and street signs, his environment keeps bombarding him with the fact of his multilingualism and his multiculturalism. To the average Filipino, this is an accepted phenomenon. The thinkers and the leaders of the nation, however, bent on harnessing all resources for national development, are studying the situation more closely.

CURRICULUM DEVELOPMENT IN ENGLISH AND PILIPINO

At this stage, after the Bilingual Education Policy was announced and before the start of its mandatory implementation in 1978, several experimental classes have been initiated to try different schemes of programing. In one school division, at least five different program schemes (described below) are being tried (7).

Scheme A. This is the scheme prescribed by the Bilingual Education Policy. Science, mathematics, and communication arts (English) are to be learned through English at the elementary and secondary levels.* All other subjects will have Pilipino as the medium of instruction.

Scheme B. This is a gradual immersion scheme. All school subjects except communication arts (English) are learned in Pilipino in the first two years of elementary school. Starting in Grade Three, there is a gradual shift to English, this being done in the mathematics first. Every year another subject is added to the English block until, in the secondary school, all subjects are taught in English, except communication arts (Pilipino).

Scheme C. This scheme aims at equal time for English and Pilipino. This time scheme starts in the fourth year of elementary school and continues in the secondary school. English is used in three subjects: science, mathematics, and communication arts (English); Pilipino is used in social studies: practical arts and Pilipino; in one subject that is composed of health, physical education, music, and scouting, both languages are used. In science and mathematics, there is a gradual shift from Pilipino to English, starting in Grade Two, with both English and Pilipino being used in mathematics. In Grade Three, science also is taught in both, with a total shift to English in mathematics. From Grade Four up, the equal time treatment is observed.

Scheme D. This is a simple maintenance program in which English is used in science, mathematics, communication arts (English), youth development training (health, physical education, music, scouting/arts); Pilipino is used in social studies and Pilipino; and both languages are used in work education.

---

*Elementary education is from Grade One to Grade Six, after which comes secondary education, which is from first year to fourth year.

GONZALEZ

Scheme E. This is a late immersion program. In Grades One to Four of the elementary school, all subjects except communication arts (English) are taught in Pilipino. In Grade Five, there is a total shift to English. All subjects, except communication arts (Pilipino) are taught in English. This total immersion continues up to the last year of secondary education.

The implementation of the policy, however, means more than just programing. It is realized that a redirection of the curriculum is necessary in the context of the new roles of the languages and the consequent time allotment for learning them. The components of the total program and the content of each should be so selected and structured as to facilitate the achievement of the goals of the bilingual education program.

THE FOREIGN LANGUAGE COMPONENT (English)

The greatly diminished time for learning English and the role that it must perform for the student calls for a new orientation in the curriculum. One linguist suggested that we streamline the syllabus, integrate, avoid duplication, and pay more attention to communication type drills and learning situations in English rather than concentrate on structure. Further, conversation must be started and kept going between the science teachers who must now begin to worry about and pay attention to linguistic problems and the teachers of English who must now worry about the conceptual problems in addition to the linguistic (8).

In the curriculum this means that science and mathematics must reinforce and further develop (reintroduce, if need be) the communication skills that have not been mastered or even introduce those that have not been taught but are necessary in learning the content of these subjects. This would require identification of the skills needed for grasping concepts successfully or for arriving at correct solutions. Since the content of science and mathematics would determine the process necessary for mastery, the specialists in these areas would need to analyze the content to determine these processes. A dialogue with the communication arts specialists should subsequently bring about the identification of skills that would need to be further developed in the content subjects. These actually provide the real situations and the real need to use the skills introduced in the communication arts.

On the other hand, the communication arts curriculum must aim not only at proficiency in the use of English, but it must also develop conceptualization skills and the general vocabulary needed for learning science and mathematics. Instructional materials need not be excerpts from the science and mathematics textbooks; they can be literary materials that will develop concepts of literature, man, and nature. This time, however, judicious selection should be exercised so that the materials will lend themselves to the development of such skills as perceiving problems, hypothesizing, categorizing, drawing conclusions, and making generalizations—so necessary in both science and mathematics. Hence, the students would be acquiring skills needed to grasp concepts in science and mathematics and not necessarily the concepts, themselves. Also, careful preparation of the materials should provide for the development of general science and mathematics vocabulary such as *height, weight, liquid, solid, planet, universe, add,* and *subtract* which can be learned in the communication arts class using general information and literature materials. A great deal of reading material would be necessary to reinforce oral learning of both linguistic and conceptualization skills. Both the curriculum writer and the teacher need to be cautioned that the development of science and mathematics as well as technical vocabulary best takes place in these classes with the teacher specialists in these areas. This is particularly true in the secondary school when the level of science concept formation becomes quite technical for the English major.

THE NATIVE LANGUAGE COMPONENT (Pilipino)

Up until the declaration of the Bilingual Education Policy, Pilipino was learned in school to express Filipino nationalism and to develop a common Filipino identity. Except for some experimental classes where it was used as the medium of instruction, Pilipino has always been a subject to be learned along with the content subjects. The effort to bring it to a more prestigious position finds expression in the policy to have it used as the medium of instruction in social studies, health, the practical arts, and physical education.

It is in this component that greater efforts are necessary since, along with the redirection of curriculum, vocabulary needed for a new register for the language would also have to be developed. Technical vocabulary for the social sciences, the practical arts, health, and physical education (at least for general education) would need to be developed. Basic concepts in diverse disciplines such as anthropology, psychology, and sociology now will have to be investigated, hypothesized, and generalized in Pilipino.

As in the English component, the communication arts curriculum must aim beyond language proficiency. It has to give training in the conceptualization processes and provide general vocabulary for content areas to be served. Likewise, the content subjects must reinforce the communication skills needed for the students to grasp concepts in these disciplines.

INTEGRATION OF THE FOREIGN AND
THE NATIVE LANGUAGE COMPONENTS

Integration does not necessarily mean the fusion of the two components since they have been neatly separated by the Philippine Bilingual Education Policy. It simply denotes the structuring of an interrelationship between the two to bring about continuity in the communication skills development of the learner. This is premised mainly on the assumption that learning two languages and using each to learn content means the same goals for the learner in the two learning experiences: acquiring the communicative systems of both languages and having them function as tools for knowledge acquisition. In both situations, therefore, the predominant learning items are communication skills; language structures or rules are learned as they are used. This connotes that every language learning activity is immediately a meaningful communication experience and that every reading activity is immediately a meaningful thinking activity, not just preparations or getting ready for language acquisition and reading in that language.

This focus on the communicative functions of language does not altogether discount the need to learn language forms. Like the first language learner, to whom, even at the earliest stages, every word learned is not just a set of phonemes but a label for something, one infused with functions (6), the school learner should be able to learn both form and meaning simultaneously through use. This direction of language learning toward the communication system is also an effort to build on commonalities rather than differences. Since any language exists and continues to exist to serve human communication, learning it involves the development of communication skills. In any language one would need to learn to perceive symbols, to discriminate, compare, and contrast as a means to using such symbols for communication. In both foreign and native languages, the learner would have to associate symbols with meanings, interpret these meanings, and further manipulate them to express his ideas or to respond to linguistic stimuli with them. This is also true of conceptualization skills. Recognizing a problem, making a hypothesis, gathering data, categorizing these, and making generalizations on them are general steps for developing science or mathematics, language or literature, social studies, and other concepts. There would, therefore, be an expected transfer of learning from one language to the other and reinforcements to be made in each, depending on the degree to which certain skills are necessary for the domains in which the language is to function.

The identification of these skills and their functional values in each of the two components would provide the basis for the building of a learning continuum. This would show how skills are to be continuously developed through an introduction-reinforcement or reintroduction-reinforcement series of activities running through the two components. This is a very important but not very easy exercise since every point plotted in the continuum represents a decision that involves analyzing a skill, determining its functional value to a learner in a specific communication situation, and anticipating when acquisition of the skill would have been completed.

Comprehension skills, for example, which are basic to any communication situation, would cover a gamut of specific skills. Listening with attention (one specific skill) has to begin on the first day of a child's school life and must continuously be reinforced in both English and Pilipino. Listening for specific sound differences may begin in one language and, if absent in the other, need not be continued in the other language. The /f-p/ difference in English words has to be learned because this makes the difference between *I saw the fool* and *I saw the pool*. While the sounds may exist in Pilipino, the difference is not a criterial attribute of the language and, therefore, need not be part of Pilipino content for learning. Listening to the difference between /i/ and /e/, however, has to be reinforced in English after having been introduced and reinforced in Pilipino, since this skill is necessary for comprehension in both languages.

For reading comprehension, picture clues are generally used. While this technique may be introduced in both languages, for word recognition, its use in Pilipino should easily move on to word clues and concept clues since the Tagalog (Pilipino) speaker even at the start of formal schooling would already have the meanings of most words in the average child's vocabulary. The development of word-picture association skills, therefore, would have to be kept going in English but need not continue too far in Pilipino.

The skill of using content clues for reading comprehension, however, would have to be reinforced continuously in both languages after it has been introduced. So vital is this vocabulary building skill to the reading process that it would have to be part of the curriculum content in both components. However, in Pilipino most of the context clues would be sentences, familiar experiences, idioms, descriptions, and examples since social studies, health, and practical arts materials would more likely have these devices. In English, much of the cluing would be through the use of the knowledge of syntax. The practice of noting phrases that serve as clues in the recognition of modified unknown words; getting the meaning of unfamiliar words through referral signals such as *these* and *same*; associating known words, parts of speech, or class words with closely related unknown words of another class; and recognizing the relationship of nonrestrictive clauses and prepositional phrases to other parts of a sentence will have to be developed more in English as a supportive measure for the reading of science and mathematics material. The use of language learning clues would then be more useful in English than the meaning learning clues, hence, reinforcement should be in this area.

This identification and sequencing of the communication skills into a learning continuum should be done, of course, with consideration of the learner and his language milieu. It is easy to build a structural content description, but to build this with an eye to the learner's psycholinguistic potentials and his sociolinguistic needs would need more than theoretical assumptions. The learner's total communication needs have to be studied so that learning can be made relevant to these needs.

THE WIDER COMMUNICATION NEEDS OF THE LEARNER

So far, the planning of the curriculum has been discussed here as it purports to serve the pedagogical needs of the learner. School, however, is time and environment bound. Any learning that takes place in school becomes really useful only as it finds application in life outside of school. Learning to use two languages is worth the investment of time and effort only if the learner is able to use both for his life needs. Such needs would direct the learning experiences in the school.

Bilingual education programs have recently been given a decidedly strong push as the civilized world becomes more and more concerned that each individual has an inherent right to be respected for his or her language and culture in any educational setting. This reality transcends any and all curricular approaches (*13*). This need gave rise to the many bilingual programs all over the world. This need gave rise to the Philippine Bilingual Education Policy of 1974.

While the nation has been bilingual/multilingual for many years now, this is the first instance when its two official languages, one native and the other foreign, will be used simultaneously as mediums of instruction throughout the whole educational system. While the motivation for learning content in Pilipino is to develop a Filipino identity through a national language and make the Filipino proud of his language and of being Filipino, it is clearly the objective to keep English in the society. This has been the expressed goal of the average Filipino parent since a knowledge of English means a chance for his children to move up the societal hierarchy. This instrumental motivation for learning English was found in at least two studies. In both studies, it was found that English is the language primarily associated with certain personal goals, directly or indirectly contributing to the individual's economic and social advancement, probably due to the prestige that English still holds as the language of most official and business transactions. English is also associated with the exchange of technical information and the use of technical terminology. One study showed that English is also the language most frequently used for reading any kind of material. The native languages are still important for most oral communication with various types of persons, whether in the home or outside. Pilipino, on the other hand, is associated primarily with citizenship and participation in the nation's affairs and is being learned to be patriotic and to understand one's heritage (*11*).

In the past few years, we have seen agitation for greater use of the national language, a general expression of the great resurgence of Filipino nationalism during those years. It has been recommended, in this regard, that more serious materials be written in Pilipino to give it greater functional value. It was predicted that soon the Filipino will exploit the advantages of his bilingualism. When he eventually becomes less self-conscious about his colonial past, a phenomenon that results in narrow nationalism, the Filipino will be proud of the fact that he belongs to a nation of mixed tongues and mixed languages (*10*).

To be relevant, the school curriculum must meet not only the school but also the wider communication needs of the students, not only the present but also the future functions of their languages. For this reason, the content of both English and Pilipino communication arts must cover general communication skills and general communication topics in the domains in which they are used. Special uses should be introduced in the communication arts class and continue to be reinforced through use in the content subjects. Hence, the foreign and native language blocks, although dichotomized on the basis of school functions, must be so organized that these, as well as the wider communication needs of the students, would direct the content of curriculum.

EVALUATION IN THE
BILINGUAL EDUCATION PROGRAM

Changed concepts of the communication arts as a component of the educational program require new concepts and processes of evaluation. Since the goal of the Philippine bilingual education policy is to produce competence in the Filipino in both English and Pilipino it is in this competence that the learner must be tested throughout the educational program. Most of this testing is done by the teachers using teacher made tests. Hence, the preservice and inservice training of teachers seeks to give them new insights into testing in the new bilingual education program. The following guidelines are being provided:

1. *Goal-test congruency.* If communication arts would now aim not only at language proficiency but also at conceptualization skills and if the content subjects would now be involved in communication skills development, tests should reflect these; otherwise the students would have to be advised that not all the processes that form the content of the different subjects will be tested.
2. *Use of a composite of measures of performance.* Both cognitive and affective domains have to be tested since the bilingual program involves both. The change of attitudes toward the languages may be tested by both objective and subjective means. Individual rating scales, fluency tests to measure speed of verbal production and verbal response, and dominance tests would measure how much the learner has accepted the use of each of his languages.

3. *Tests of integrative skills.* These would better reflect language proficiency (Oller and Richards) and would test total language use, not discrete language skills. The items generally require complete responses to verbal stimuli or composition type answers which students write on given topics. They test not only proficiency but the development of thinking skills.
4. *The use of two languages for testing.* Both English and Pilipino will eventually be used for testing communication skills. Teachers have not started—as transition measures—to write their lesson plans, discuss lessons, and give tests in Pilipino. By 1981, it is expected that the Filipino can take his examinations in either language.

These are transition years for all in the country and decisions are being made along the way to make the present curriculum reflect the educational goals. The teachers are being involved through seminars and workshops; other agencies and sectors are being called in to participate in the major decisions that would still need to be made. Hopefully, the Filipino can keep and exploit his bilingualism to the fullest for his as well as the society's progress and development. This is to be supported by a curriculum that is sensitive to both the learner's and society's need for more than one language.

References

1. Cohen, Andrew D. *A Sociolinguistic Approach to Bilingual Education.* Rowley, Massachusetts: Newbury House, 1975.
2. Constantino, Renato. *The Filipinos in the Philippines.* Manila: Malaya Books, 1966.
3. Corpus, Onofre D. *The Philippines.* Englewood Cliffs, New Jersey: Prentice-Hall, 1965.
4. Department of Education and Culture. *Implementing Guidelines for the Policy on Bilingual Education,* Department Order No. 25. Manila, 1974.
5. Department of Education and Culture. *Annual Report.* Manila: Population Education Center, 1974.
6. Diggory, Sylvia Farnham. *Cognitive Processes in Education.* New York: Harper and Row, 1972.
7. Division of City Schools, *Bilingual Programs,* Department Order No. 25. Manila: s. 1974, 1976.
8. Gonzalez, Andrew. *"The New Bilingual Education Policy in Non-Tagalog Speaking Areas,"* speech delivered at the First Joint National Conference-Workshop for Language Supervisors of the Philippines, Silay City, May 1975.
9. Gonzalez, Esperanza. *A Framework for the English Curriculum of the Philippine Secondary Schools.* Manila: University of Santo Tomas, 1973.
10. Goulet, Rosalina Morales. *Bilingualism in the Philippine Setting.* Quezon City: Souvenir Publications, 1974.
11. Otanes, Fe T., and Bonifacio Sibayan. *Language Policy Survey of the Philippines.* Manila: Language Study Center, Philippine Normal College, 1969.
12. Presidential Commission to Survey Philippine Education. *Education for National Development, New Pattern, New Direction.* Manila: Philippine Commission to Survey Philippine Education. *Education for National Development, New Pattern, New Direction.* Manila: Philippine Commission to Survey Philippine Education, 1970.
13. Ramos, T.V., and E.A. Gonzalez. *Bilingualism and Bilingual Education.* Quezon City: Cultural Publications, 1975.
14. Ramos, et al. *Philippine Language Policy.*
15. Rice, Frank (Ed.). *Study of the Role of Second Language in Asia, Africa, and Latin America,* Washington, D.C.: Center for Applied Linguistics, 1962.
16. Vigil, Dennis, and Donald Moore. "A Perspective for Bilingual/Bicultural Education," paper from Denver and Greely, Colorado Foundations' Follow through Program.

Issues in the Teaching of English as a Second Language in Malaysia

Lim Kiat Boey
University of Malaya
Kuala Lumpur
Malaysia

Malaysia is a multiracial, multilingual country, the three major races being Malay, Chinese, and Indian. Discounting the dialects one may say there are three languages, but historical accident has added English to the languages used regularly.

English education has endured for more than one hundred years in Malaysia, beginning with the establishment of Penang Free School in 1816. After World War II and with the achievement of independence in 1957, the national system of education continued to provide education in the English medium. Primary schools offered six-year courses in four languages (Malay, English, Chinese, and Tamil). Secondary education in fully-assisted schools was at first offered only in the English medium, but owing to popular demand it was also provided in the Malay medium from 1956. A number of Chinese medium secondary schools received partial aid until 1961, after which they had to change their medium of instruction to Malay or English in order to qualify for government financial aid. Where pupils had a change of medium in going from primary to secondary schools, they spent an extra year in a "Remove Class" to raise their level of attainment in the medium of instruction. This provision was made only for those going into the English medium secondary schools until 1976 when Malay Remove Classes were started. English was and is taught as a subject in all non-English medium schools.

Tables 1 and 2 show the enrollment in schools of various media in the years 1947-1969.*

Table 1

	Primary			
Medium	1947	1957	1967	1969
Malay	164,528	441,567	591,560	603,410
English	45,174	130,360	289,056	326,306
Chinese	139,191	310,458	355,771	378,679
Tamil	33,954	50,766	79,203	80,750

Table 2

	Secondary			
Medium	1947	1957	1967	1969
Malay**	-	2,315	128,069	134,889
English	12,510	48,235	286,254	333,927
Chinese***	2,692	30,052	-	-
Tamil	93	440	-	-

**Secondary education in the Malay medium started in 1956.
***Assisted secondary education in Chinese stopped in 1961.

It will be seen that by 1969 the increase in enrollment for Malay, Chinese, and Tamil medium schools had diminished in comparison with that for English medium schools. Apparently, in spite of the constitution and national pride in political independence, the value of English education continued to attract more and more children into the English medium schools. But if Malay is to be in fact (and not only in the constitution) the national language, then the trend must be stopped or reversed. A decision taken by the Ministry of Education in that year was soon to change the picture.

At the time of achieving independence, it was written into the constitution that Malay would be the national language and English the official second language. It was also decided that a transition period of ten years (1957-1967) would be allowed during which there would be a gradual switch from the use of English to Malay for

*The figures were obtained from *Educational Statistics of Malaysia 1938-1967*; Ministry of Education, Malaysia, 1967; and Baharuddin Musa and Shaharuddin Harun, *Situation of Children and Youth in West Malaysia*, Prime Minister's Department, 1970.

administration and education. It turned out that the changeover in language use was not proceeding at the anticipated pace for the nationalists, who were understandably impatient to express their independence from a language that reminded them of their erstwhile subservience. Their agitations resulted in firmer steps being taken to ensure that Malay supersede English in administration and education. In the latter sphere, the policy of withdrawing English as a medium of instruction was adopted.

Beginning with Standard One in 1970 and every year going one grade up the educational ladder, Malay would replace English as the medium of instruction although Chinese and Tamil medium primary schools were allowed to continue. This means that, by 1982, all secondary education up to preuniversity classes would be taught in Malay. Higher education would have to follow suit. In actual practice, Malay has already become the medium of instruction at the universities. Another decision toward strengthening the position of the national language was to replace the Cambridge School Certificate from 1970 with the Malaysian Certificate of Education (or MCE), for which a pass was compulsory in Malay but not in English. The equivalent certificate in Malay (the Sijil Pelajaran Malaysia or SPM) also requires a pass in Malay but not in English. This means that, in the classroom, English would be given less weight by the pupils, if not by their teachers.

It is not surprising that there should be ambivalence in the official attitudes toward English as a second language. While the spirit of nationalism and national pride call for the use of the national language, the need for English as the language of international communication and for science and technology cannot be denied. Hence, while the authorities and the media expand the use of the national language as a sign of the people's loyalty and as a tool to forge national unity, the importance of learning English and of maintaining the standard of English is reiterated in speeches at various school functions and at seminars. And yet, dropping the required pass in English from the school leaving examination (in an examination conscious school system) is bound to militate against the maintenance of standards. Educationists have advised that some subjects be taught in English as a means of maintaining the level of English but to no avail. This is just another case of political expedience being at odds with educational wisdom. To reintroduce English as a medium of instruction, even if only for subjects like physical education and domestic science, is unthinkable at this juncture. National development and solidarity must be given priority at any cost. National pride is also at stake.

It appears that each emerging nation has to go through its own growing pains with regard to language. It is not enough to experience vicariously the linguistic vicissitudes of our near neighbours like Ceylon and India. Perhaps when Malay is indubitably established as the national language and is proudly demonstrated to be adequate for the expression of every aspect of life in the country, then the leaders and citizenry may feel confident enough to experiment with allowing one or two subjects to be taught in English. The repeated admonition, at public functions, to study English well is not mere lip service to the country's official second language. The desire to maintain the standard of English is sincere enough, but the timing is not yet right for politicians and educationists to operate on the same wavelength on every matter of educational import.

While the role of English in school is changing from being one medium of instruction to that of being a subject only (albeit a compulsory one for every pupil), the stated aims of teaching English seem to have been changed little. A quick glance at the English syllabuses written before the seventies shows that scant attention was paid to the statement of aims. For example, the 1959 syllabus for non-English medium primary schools makes no reference at all to the aims of teaching English. By implication, all the four skills are to be taught since there are sections on oral English, reading, and written English. The English syllabus for English medium secondary schools makes a single, global statement of aims:

> This syllabus is a continuation of the syllabus for Primary Schools and aims at giving the pupils—through the skills of writing, listening with understanding, reading and speaking—a complete mastery of the essential structures of the English Language and of additional vocabulary and idioms.*

When syllabus committees were appointed to rewrite the English syllabuses for the seventies, they asked the Ministry of Education for an official statement of aims for teaching English to guide them in their deliberations. They felt that this was necessary since the role of English was changing not only in school but also in society at large. Since the use of English would diminish, should the syllabuses emphasize the

---

*Published as G.N. 897 in the Malaysia Government Gazette, March 11, 1965.

receptive skills of listening and reading and give less importance to the productive skills of speaking and writing? Many felt that reading should be given most emphasis because it was not only in tertiary education that books and journals mostly would be in English but also, in everyday life, recreational and instructional materials tend to be richer and more abundant in English than in the other major languages used in Malaysia.

However, the statement of aims that was issued made no differential emphasis on the four skills. The importance of each skill was merely explicitly stated where it had been implied before. The statement is given in full below.

> In line with the National Educational policy, English is to be taught as an effective second language in Malaysian schools. The following sets of terminal competence may be expected of the student.
>
> A. At the end of his Primary Education:
> i) To have oral and aural skills of a level where simple English may be used correctly in a variety of situations.
> ii) To understand and be able to enjoy simple written English, once given an adequate vocabulary and a range of structures.
> iii) To write legibly and effectively for simple and informal written communication.
> B. At the end of his lower Secondary Education:
> i) To display oral and aural skills containing a larger number of patterns and an extended vocabulary in a variety of situations.
> ii) In reading to be able to extract the gist of a passage, the stated and inferrable details, cause and effect relationships, comparisons and character traits; to classify, outline, and sequence ideas and to predict outcomes.
> iii) To be able to produce a unified piece of writing that displays structural correctness and a sense of purpose as well as the development of a theme or idea, to record accurately and concisely notes on what is read and heard.
> C. At the end of his Secondary Education (Form Five):
> i) To communicate effectively and be internationally intelligible in his speech.
> ii) To understand any form of recreational or instructional material relevant to his stage of learning.
> iii) To be able to write effectively and with precision for different purposes.

This statement of policy is in line with the aforesaid admonition to maintain the standard of English in spite of its changed role in the educational system. It has had certain repercussions on the content of syllabuses and the amount of time allocated to English on the timetable. The effects on the syllabus may be most clearly demonstrated in the latest English syllabus for Forms 4 and 5. Since standards must be maintained, it is assumed that the syllabus must prepare pupils to meet the same needs as they met at a time when English was the sole official language. As a result, there is a tendency to include too much and, consequently, to claim more time on the timetable for English, but the allocation of time is not uniform for Malay medium and non-Malay medium schools.

The exposure time to English is much less in non-Malay medium primary schools, yet the students are expected to follow the same syllabus. The discrepancy is expected to be made up for in the extra year in the English Remove Class, but the fact remains that there is no equivalence. In view of this discrepency and the changing role of English, some educationists have thought it might be worth reconsidering the optimal time for starting English in the Malaysian educational system. There are two possibilities: 1) to start everyone, regardless of medium of instruction, in English in the third year of school (at age eight) and 2) to start English in the first year of secondary school (at age twelve).

Administratively, there are some advantages for both starting times. At present, the country has a great shortage of teachers trained to teach English. The shortage is particularly acute in primary schools and in rural areas. Putting off the teaching of English for a few years will ease problems engendered by the shortage of teachers. It will also temporarily solve the problem of the shortage of teaching materials. Starting everyone at a uniform time will obviate the complaints of parents (and teachers) that the Chinese and Tamil medium pupils are at a disadvantage, since they have to do in five years what the Malay medium pupils do in six and with a more generous time allocation per week. A uniform starting time makes possible a uniform allocation of time for English in schools of all media.

In the context of a shortage of teachers and materials, it may also be educationally sounder to start later. When untrained teachers (or trained teachers whose command of English is not up to standard) are assigned to teach English, the result is poor attainment in the subject on the part of pupils. When the examination results of pupils who started English in the first year and those who started in the third year were compared, it was found that there was no statistically significant difference between them. It has been argued that the generally poor English results in primary schools may be partly due to the pupils' having to cope with too many languages as soon as they enter school.

Would it not be better to let them get firmly established in the medium of instruction first? Once they have learned to communicate confidently in the language of instruction (which may not be their home language), they may be able to concentrate on learning English. It is true that children are able to pick up two or three languages simultaneously in informal contexts of play, but language learning in the classroom is a different matter. First, instruction is formal and, second, there is no real motivation since the need to communicate can already be satisfied in the first language.

Postponing the study of English to the secondary school would be a more radical change in educational policy, though it is common practice in school systems in the West where FLES (Foreign Languages in the Elementary Schools) is a recent innovation. Those who would drop English out of the primary school argue that at that level it is difficult for the pupils to see the relevance of the subject. They are too far away from the world of work and higher education to realise the importance of English in their lives. The advocates also say that the level of achievement after four or six years of English is not commensurate with the time spent and, in any case, the syllabus items have to be revised or taught again in the lower secondary school. It is also argued that since the pupils are more mature, given a more intensive course, they would be able to cover in the three years of the lower secondary school what is now done in the primary and lower secondary schools.

The advocates of introducing English in secondary schools only tend also to be those who think that the emphasis of English in Malaysian schools should be on the reading skill. For this reason, the advantage argued for an early start in order to achieve a more native-like accent is not in question. It is pertinent to note, however, that a more intensive course at this level would create administrative problems, since more time must be found for English in an already overcrowded timetable. Also, although all pupils are entitled to nine years of education, not all go beyond the primary school and the dropouts would miss English altogether.

What do theory and research have to say on the subject of the optimal time to start second language learning? According to Lenneberg's "critical period" theory, language acquisition is directly related to the maturation process and the critical period extends from ages two to thirteen (or the early teens). During the critical period, readiness for language acquisition tends to be synchronised with physical maturation and growth. Lenneberg's observations of aphasic patients showed that lateralisation is flexible in the critical period but becomes fixed in the early teens. However, Krashen (6) adduced some evidence that the developmental course of lateralization is not associated with Lenneberg's proposed critical period and that first language learning is possible after puberty.

If we hold with Lenneberg's suggestion (7) of the critical period with regard to first language acquisition, then, "it seems that the critical period is important for second language learning in that a matrix of language skills is fixed by the end of the period. Second languages learned during the critical period should be achieved with less effort than languages learned after the matrix is set" (5:281). In this case, starting English in the third year (at eight years of age) would appear more in line with the neurolinguistic development of human beings than starting in the secondary school.

When we look at research for guidance in this matter of the optimal age for starting a second language, the findings are either conflicting or inconclusive. Asher's study (2) on pronunciation comparing adults and children showed that age of starting and duration of study are the best predictors of native-like pronunciation. The earlier the starting age and the longer the period of study, the more native-like the pronunciation. On the other hand, in a study by Asher and Price (1) on listening comprehension of Russian, the adults were greatly superior to the children in any age group (ages seven, eleven, and fourteen) and the older children were better than the youngest children. Asher (2:341) concluded, "It may be that different types of learning are operating. Pronunciation may be a learning based on copying while listening comprehension may be learning rules and principles."

There have been many experiments in FLES in western countries but the results are inconclusive and not readily comparable because, as Carroll (4) pointed out, there are differences in the languages learned, motivation for learning the second language, relative status of the first and second language, opportunity to learn, and mode of learning.

In France, Germany, and Sweden, where English is taught as a second language, there have been attempts to find the best starting age. In France (9:56-57) primary schools have experimented with the teaching of English since 1956. They have found the best starting age to be year two of primary school (pupils aged eight to nine). In Germany, systematic experiments in the teaching of a foreign language to younger children began in 1960. It had been customary to begin the teaching of English from the first year of secondary school and the fifth year of the elementary school upwards. They experimented with starting in the third year of schooling or when the child was nine-years-old. According to the report, "the early start is valuable, but whether it justifies a reorganisation of current practice for all schools, i.e. that English should generally be started in the third year instead of later, is still an open question" (9:60-61.) In Sweden, the starting age for a foreign language was ten. In 1957, experimentation began with starting at age seven. "The results of the Swedish experiment are difficult to interpret. They seem to suggest that starting a language without a book at seven is either too early or too late.... An analysis of tests, however, administered in 1958 had led to the conclusion that 'pronunciation as well as understanding improved more rapidly the older the pupils were. Pupils of eleven years of age learnt more accurately and rapidly than seven year olds.'" (9:44).

Discounting the variables indicated by Carroll, we may draw certain conclusions regarding the optimal starting age for Malaysia. None of the countries we have discussed even considered the first year of primary school for starting a second language. This speaks against the wisdom of starting English in Standard I, especially when we remember that those countries are monolingual, whereas Malaysia is multilingual. The favourable age is between year eight and eleven. In our school system, this means between Standard III and VI. Starting in Standard III gives two years for the child to get established in the language of instruction and a good four years of English for the child who drops out at the end of primary school, so that he need not be deprived of the educational benefits of learning a second language. Whether the children are really more ready to learn English in the third year of school than in the first year will have to be settled by extended experiment.

Another issue in TESL in Malaysia is the place of ESP (English for Special Purposes). At the tertiary level of education, ESP has long been accepted as necessary. At every language unit or centre of universities where English is taught, materials are being prepared to cater to the needs of students in the various disciplines, particularly EST (English for Science and Technology). It is assumed by the university authorities that what the students need to develop is reading skill in English, since they need to read books and journals which are largely in English. Another assumption is that practice with the kind of materials they have to cope with in their respective disciplines helps them to improve rapidly. It is true that they need to read and that the reading of the kind of materials made familiar through practice is facilitated, but the writer's experience with undergraduates who learn English seems to indicate that they not only want to be able to read but, also, to speak English. The latter ability confers a certain prestige and improves their chances in the job market. Also, giving them a fare of nothing but materials related to their disciplines produces boredom. They prefer a variety of reading passages to maintain interest.

How far down or up the school system ESP should be introduced is debatable. The English taught in schools is common core English. It has been claimed by some writers of the latest communicational syllabus that it is essentially ESP based, but the claim has not been substantiated by specifying the structures required for the various purposes for which English is used. It is a rather loose use of the term ESP. A more valid claim is made for an EST course in the science classes of residential schools. This is an experimental course devised by two British volunteer teachers. It seems to have had some success with the students, who are all Malays. But the question to be decided is whether the EST course is to be used in addition to the common core English course, in which case more time would have to be found in the already crowded timetable, or the ESR course is to replace the common core course. In the end, it was decided to combine the two and to extend the experiment beyond the two residential schools to other science residential schools.

The issues discussed in this paper include the official attitude towards English as a second language, the aims of teaching English in a changing environment, the optimal age of starting English, and the place of ESP.

References

1. Asher, J.J., and B. Price. "The Learning Strategy of the Total Physical Response: Some Age Differences," *Child Development*, 38 (1967), 1219-1227.
2. Asher, J.J. "The Optional Age to Learn a Foreign Language," *Modern Language Journal*, 53 (1969), 334-341.
3. Baharuddin, Musa, and Shaharuddin Harun. *Situations of Children and Youth in West Malaysia.* Prime Minister's Department, 1970.
4. Carroll, J.B. "Research Problems Concerning the Teaching of Foreign or Second Languages to Younger Children," in H.H. Stern (Ed.), *Foreign Languages in Primary Education.* New York: Oxford University Press, 1967.

5. Hepaworth, J.C. "The Importance and Implication of the Critical Period for Second Language Learning," *English Language Teaching*, 28 (1975), 272-282.
6. Krashen, Stephen D. "Lateralization, Language Learning, and the Critical Period: Some New Evidence," *Language Learning*, 23 (1973), 63-74.
7. Lenneberg, Eric H. *Biological Foundations of Language*. New York: John Wiley, 1967.
8. Ministry of Education, Malaysia. *Educational Statistics of Malaysia, 1938-1967.*
9. Stern, H.H. (Ed.). *Foreign Languages in Primary Education*. New York: Oxford University Press, 1967.

Problems and Progress in Teaching English as a Foreign Language in Indonesia

Eugenius Sadtono
Institute of Education
Malang, Indonesia

INTRODUCTION

English as a foreign language has become an historical linguistic phenomenon in Indonesia. As a foreign language, it has seen three eras of history: Dutch, Japanese, and Indonesian. The historical development is presented here so that we can see how it progresses from just "one of those foreign languages" into the first foreign language, though we do not want it to become *the* second language.

To acquire a foreign language in a developing country such as Indonesia is probably rather different from acquiring one in a developed country; but the difference lies mostly in the nonlinguistic aspects. The linguistic aspects are, generally speaking, universal.

There is, of course, some progress made in the use of English by society in Indonesia. But whether the progress has any correlation with the formal teaching of English in our schools remains to be seen. The progress of English as a foreign language in our society is manifested in a number of forms to be presented later. In academic circles, however, the feeling is that there is much decline in the results of TEFL. Part of the blame actually lies in the Ministry of Education which tackles the TEFL problems whimsically and sporadically.

The Dutch Period (1700-1942)

The Dutch, being from a small nation in Europe, have to learn other major European languages well if they are to communicate with other neighboring countries for survival. Proximity with England is an advantage to those learning English, as they can visit England easily and practice the language. The Dutch tradition of learning and mastering a foreign language well was also brought to Indonesia. Therefore, the Dutch teachers of English had really mastered English and were competent teachers. Even if they employed the old grammar translation method, they themselves were good models when they taught oral English. It was during this time that the teaching of English in Indonesia could be labeled "successful"; that is, high school graduates could read English books more or less with ease. Their success was due to several factors.

In addition to excellent training in the Netherlands, Dutch ability to speak English was a good stimulus to motivate their students to master English. Being Dutch nationals, the teachers received a very good salary and could concentrate wholeheartedly on their work.

At that time, there were insufficient schools to permit most Indonesians to have even a primary education. Most of the people were illiterate. The relatively few public schools were reserved for the royal family and for children of indigenous officials. The few sectarian and nonsectarian private secondary schools, by and large, were maintained either for the Chinese, Arab, and Indian minority groups or for the same population as the public schools. English was taught in many of the secondary schools, but very few indigenous children attended these schools. Generally speaking, the students were the children of the cream of society who were understandably well-nourished and, therefore, more highly motivated and intelligent than the other children. Textbooks, reading books, and visual aids were complete and easily available. Classrooms were good and the number of students was small.

Students who entered the secondary school would really have mastered oral and written Dutch, as all the lessons in the elementary school were given in Dutch. This mastery of Dutch (a Germanic language akin to English, sharing similar Western weltanschauung) accounted for their success in learning English, as the transfer from Dutch to English was less difficult than, say, Javanese to English.

The Japanese Period (1942-1945)

During the World War II years of conflict, the school system was much disrupted. Whenever possible, the schools continued to meet but, generally, had to operate with a reduced staff and to suspend their sessions for various reasons for days and weeks at a time. Under the Japanese administration, the schools were forbidden to teach English, though some private instruction in English continued clandestinely. The use of Dutch was also strictly prohibited. Instead, the Japanese imposed their own language, and Indonesian was officially introduced as the national language. It was a real setback for the teaching of English in Indonesia, and the birth of Indonesian as the national language would later become one of the major obstacles for the success of English in Indonesia.

The Independence (1945 to the present)

When the Dutch attempted to reassume control of the colony after the war, they also attempted to reopen the schools with essentially the same curricula as before the war. Dutch teachers were brought in, and positions were also offered to those indigenous teachers who had taught before the war and others who had qualified since, provided they had not committed themselves openly to the independence movement.

However, this Indonesian independence movement, which had grown rapidly during the war and established a republic, prevented the Dutch from realizing their plans.

When the Dutch retreated, the Indonesian government decided early that Dutch was no longer acceptable. The grounds for this decision were twofold: 1) Dutch is the language of the former colonial authority which relinquished this authority only after years of violent war, and 2) Dutch is used only by the people of the Netherlands and the Dutch colonies—it has no international currency. But they did not intend to replace Dutch with any other foreign language; the national language of Indonesia was to be Indonesian, a Malayo-Polynesian language closely similar to Malay, which began as a lingua franca for the Dutch East Indies.

Insofar as Dutch would be replaced by any foreign language at all, it was decided that language would be English. But English would not take the place of Dutch, except in a very limited way. English would not become a second language for Indonesia, it would be the first foreign language. In most respects, a second language occupies a position equal to the first language. A first foreign language does not occupy any such position, it is the language which will be expected to be used only where circumstances make it infeasible to use the national language.

The following is a quotation from a statement by Frits Wachendorff, the first head of the Central Inspectorate of English Language Instruction in the Ministry of Education:

> What then is the objective of English teaching in Indonesia? This is a question we have to answer first before we can start the discussions on the proposed curriculum. Some five years ago when the Kursus BI-Bahasa Inggris was first established we had only vague ideas about what could be the aim of the teaching of English in the Indonesian schools. Consequently, false assumptions regarding the function of English in the Indonesian Educational System were circulating and remained unchecked. Some people believed that English was a replacement for Dutch, others thought that it was to be the second language in Indonesia. As time progressed, it became clearer and clearer that it was neither. The rapid development of Bahasa Indonesia gave the solution of the vernacular language. Today it has proved itself capable of serving the national needs to a remarkably wide extent, both as a language of administration and as a medium of science instruction. This put the replacement of Dutch by another foreign language out of the question.
>
> It is not difficult to see that English can never be a second language in Indonesia either. Most of the Indonesian children begin their linguistic experience with one of the regional languages. So, in terms of language learning, the Bahasa Indonesia is their second language. As for its function, English is not and will never be a social language in the Indonesian community. Neither is it nor will it be the second official language in the administration of this country. It is no more and no less than the "first foreign language."
>
> This being clear we can now try to explain and define the objective of English learning in the Indonesian schools. As I said before, the development of the Bahasa Indonesia is such that it can be used satisfactorily as the medium of instruction at all levels of education in this country. However, up till now very few books have been written in this language for the academic level of training and we still have to make use of foreign lecturers at the universities. This means that we have to make the common treasure of science and wisdom available to our young men and women through a foreign language. That English is chosen for this purpose is a matter of practical insight. Being a universal language, it is also suitable to serve the Indonesian interest in other fields, as for instance the communication with other peoples. After this explanation it is easy to see that the objective of English teaching in our schools is primarily utilitarian.
>
> What does this objective imply? It implies that the task of the secondary school is to equip the pupils with a "working knowledge" of English and not with just a smattering of the language plus a lot of useless theory about it. It implies that the secondary school has to teach the pupils to use the language (4).

The educated people of the older generation always complain that present high school graduates cannot read, let alone speak, English whereas earlier students could at least read and comprehend English books when they graduated from their high schools. The older generation claimed they had already mastered Dutch after graduating from the elementary school and Dutch was more difficult than English. Their judgment was, understandably, unfair. The following are some of the reasons why.

GENERAL REASONS

Universal Education and Increase of Population

The explosive increases in population and universal education (available to everyone regardless of social class) do not compare with the situation in the Dutch era. The two factors have made classrooms overcrowded (average size, 45 students to a class) and teaching language a difficult task to execute, whatever method is applied. In addition, the students come from different social classes with different backgrounds; in other words, they do not come from the cream of society as they did in the Dutch era. This heterogeneous mixture of students naturally lowers the possibility of success in teaching language.

Social Reasons

In the Dutch era, people who spoke Dutch felt they had ascended one step in the ladder of society belonging to the upper or upper-middle class. In other words, the ability to speak Dutch was a status symbol. It was true that people who could speak—not necessarily read—Dutch were regarded as being "educated" and therefore gained more respect. In addition, those who mastered Dutch had a better chance in job seeking and job promotion than those who did not. Therefore, people were highly motivated to acquire Dutch.

The situation now is different; English is not completely regarded as a status symbol. Educated people do realize the importance of English for international communication and scientific purposes, but the general public does not see any immediate benefits from mastering English. Indonesian is sufficient for immediate benefits and enjoyment.

Native Speakers

In the Dutch period, Dutch native speakers were numerous, and Indonesians who adopted Dutch as their first or native tongue were uncountable. For example, the people in North Sulawesi and South Maluku virtually adopted Dutch as their native tongue. Therefore, immediate opportunity to use Dutch was always available.

On the other hand, the immediate opportunity to use English is very seldom (if ever) found, except in the big cities. English native speakers are very few indeed and, therefore, people who learn English using the audiolingual method have practically no chance to use it with native speakers. If motivation is high at first, it usually dwindles because the opportunity to practice English is very slim.

The following situation is an example of immediate benefit of knowing English. In the island of Bali where tourists are abundant—mostly native speakers of English—the peddlers and owners of art shops can communicate in English (probably Pidgin English) without much difficulty, whereas most of them are illiterate.

Reading Materials

Such books and magazines were abundant and cheap during the Dutch period, and the economy was good; therefore, people could afford to buy them. Books and magazines in the indigenous language were very few. This situation motivated people even more to master Dutch.

English magazines and books are not abundant and they are expensive, so only a few people can afford to buy them. The only English magazines now obtainable are *Time, Newsweek, Asiaweek,* and *Reader's Digest*, which are available only in big cities.

Indonesian books and magazines are now abundant. This is certainly one psychological reason why English fails to succeed. People are reluctant to work hard to master English, particularly when they can already enjoy books and magazines in Indonesian. After all, a considerable number of articles printed in Indonesian magazines are translations from English magazines. Good as well as bad stories are available in Indonesian. In the Dutch period, it was difficult to find a pornographic book in any of the indigenous languages in Indonesia. One had to master Dutch to enjoy either really good books or really voyeuristic or pornographic books. Today, there is not the same sense of urgency to learn English as there was to learn Dutch during the Dutch era.

Competition with Indonesian Language

In the Dutch era, Dutch was second to none and the language virtually encompassed every aspect of social communication, life, pleasure, and education. Development of Indonesian was severely affected.

Indonesian now is fully capable of replacing Dutch in practically all aspects of life. The reintroduction of English as the first foreign language is theoretically sound, but success is doubtful. Sociologically speaking, at the moment, Indonesian people do not perceive any immediate use or benefit from learning English. Motivation to study English will never be the same as the earlier motivation to learn Dutch. It is true that quite a few university textbooks are still available in English and Dutch, but most of the students are happy with the ones in Indonesian. When they have to read other textbooks, they ask their friends from the English department to translate them or summarize them in Indonesian. Only graduate students in science do their best to read English textbooks, as very few texts have been translated into Indonesian.

A proposal to teach English in the elementary schools met with strong opposition from a big section of the public who fear that English may replace Indonesian in the long run—a not uncommon fear among developing nations with rather chauvinistic attitudes.

The tragic result of the decreasing quality of the teaching of English in Indonesia can be observed from the following facts:

- In 1968, only 45 out of 400 university graduates applying for AID scholarships could pass the English test.
- A number of scholarships offered to university lecturers by English speaking countries cannot be filled because of applicants' poor proficiency in English.
- Otherwise capable university graduates failed to secure jobs with foreign companies due to poor performance in English.

The Curriculum

Is English really needed in Indonesian high schools and universities? If so, to what extent is it needed? What percentage of graduates really need English?

The answers to such questions depend on a number of factors. If we want to be realistic, major factors are social and geographical, particularly urban versus rural needs. English is definitely not needed in the rural areas: therefore, the first step to make TEFL more effective is to limit it to the urban areas.

How many high school and university students really need English? If the percentage is small, the best thing to do is to offer English as an elective subject, or to offer it to those who are going to continue their study at the university. Such a step would be much more efficient and economical than the present system which presumes that everybody needs English. This view may be against the educational philosophy that everyone should be given equal opportunity to study English. Or if the educational policy is to teach English so that students understand other people's cultural backgrounds, then leave things as they are.

The next issue is, "If English is needed in the urban areas by a particular group of students, what is the main objective?" If we can answer that question, then we can design our curriculum more clearly and meaningfully.

The English curriculum of high school as well as the university is not clearly spelled out. In relation to time allotment and teaching materials, the objectives are vague, too ambitious, and unrealistic. A high school graduate, for example, is supposed to be able to read textbooks and listen to lectures delivered in English. It takes us three years to train our students in the English Department of the Institute of Education to reach the same objective—and these students are virtually the cream of high school graduates.

Another major weakness is the absence of any standard measurement. If we had our objectives clearly spelled out, we would still need an instrument to measure whether our students had really achieved the objectives. The nonexistence of a national standardized test destroys motivation of the teacher as well as the student. The standardized test would make the teacher feel responsible if the majority of students fail in the test. The student, too, would feel more secure with a clear objective to achieve.

Another disadvantage of the nonexistence of a standardized test is that we can never really evaluate the program and progress in TEFL. The results of a reliable test could be employed to evaluate the program as well as compare generations of graduates.

Materials

Teaching materials are now available, but the supply is insufficient. There are not enough books for general reading for the elementary and intermediate levels, materials essential for developing student motivation to pursue the study of English.

The application of visual aids has never been seriously exploited, except for some junior high schools using the audiolingual method. In the senior high school, visual aids are not used as the students are supposed to have mastered elementary English, and the teacher thinks they do not need them anymore.

Audio aids, such as the tape recorder and the record player, are not used, except in the English Department of the Teacher College of the State University. The reasons are simple: 1) it is very expensive to set up a good language laboratory, 2) secondary school teachers cannot afford to buy tape recorders, and 3) they do not know how to use tape recorders effectively. The language laboratory in particular is very costly to maintain, and the spare parts are not easily available in Indonesia; as a result, some of the language laboratories lay idle.

Hours

Junior High School. At present the method being tried is basically the audiolingual method. If it is to be successful, the method requires a considerable amount of class hours, small classes, sufficient materials, and competent teachers. The materials themselves are scientifically satisfactory, but the other conditions are far from ideal. Average class hours amount to four a week. The average class size is 45 students, and often a desk for two students is occupied by three. Quite a few of the classrooms are poorly partitioned and the loud voices—particularly during drills—from one room always disturb another. In the big cities, materials are fairly sufficient, but in small towns they are not. It is likely that less than 50 percent of the teachers are competent, and very few of them can speak English.

Senior High School. The goal in the senior high school is teaching students to read English. There is no uniformity in methodology, but the majority of the teachers apply the grammar-translation method. The general condition of the senior high school is not any better than that of the junior high school: overcrowded classes, small number of hours, poor classrooms, and poor materials. Most of the teachers, however, are relatively competent as approximately 65 percent of them are college graduates. Competent English teachers are few in comparison with teachers of other subjects, and they are usually in great demand. Consequently, they usually teach at several different schools to meet demands and, also, to make both ends meet. Such a situation is not at all favorable to the students, as the teachers are overburdened and concentrate less on each class.

Vocational School. The situation at the vocational school is much worse, as English is taught only perfunctorily for two hours a week. As both teacher and students realize that it is only a secondary subject, they are not enthusiastic about learning. The result is quite predictable: very poor knowledge of English.

University. At the university in general (except the English Department), English is offered perfunctorily—that is, two hours a week in the freshman year. The goal of English teaching here is that students gain reading ability in their major field. The goal, however, is never attainable due to the following:

- Classes are oversized (from 20-200 students) and are not broken down into small classes, due to shortage of room.
- There is an incredibly wide range of English backgrounds among the students.
- The allotted period is much too short: 64 hours a year (2 hours per school week).

Fortunately, some universities now realize the faults and have made an attempt to improve instruction by adding more hours per week and lengthening the period (instead of instruction during the freshman year only, they extend it to the senior year).

PROGRESS

On one hand, there is considerable progress in terms of the availability of materials; but, on the other hand, there is a decline in the quality of student achievement in general. A host of factors contribute to the decline in achievement. Among these are the growth of Bahasa Indonesia (the national language) which pervades all walks of life, insufficient time allotment, and oversize classes.

Progress in EFL in Indonesia can be observed from the following facts: more time allotment for high schools, more textbooks and supplementary readers, more training centers for government officials going overseas to study, encouragement given to government as well as private company officials to take up English courses, crash programs to train teachers of English for junior and senior high schools (a one-year course), the use of TV, the increasing numbers of private courses, and the easy availability of English magazines and newspapers. I should like to discuss the last two items in particular.

Private courses and English magazines offer reliable checks as to whether EFL has really made progress. Private courses reflect the needs of society, either economical or social. If the number of private courses increases, it means that the demand is high. The high demand may be caused by economical necessities (getting a job, promotion) or social motives (status symbol, overseas travel as a tourist). Whether these private courses are successful in producing people who can use English is a different question.

The increase of sales of English magazines (*Reader's Digest, Time, Newsweek, Asiaweek*) is probably a better indicator of whether EFL has been successful. People do not want to waste money buying a magazine they cannot read. If *Newsweek* has a special publication for Indonesia, it definitely means that more Indonesians can read English (though, of course, it also caters to expatriates living in Indonesia). Whether it is a result of formal schooling or otherwise is anybody's guess.

EVALUATION OF THE PRESENT EFFORTS

The Ministry of Education is very much concerned with the teaching of English, as evidenced in some projects of training English teachers and the preparation of instructional materials. Assistance in English instruction was sought from the governments, private educational organizations and philanthropic organizations of the English speaking countries. The United States Government provided experts to assist with inservice training, beginning August 1952. The British Council conducted similar training and then switched to assistance in the universities. A number of Australian college graduates volunteered to assist the English Language Teacher Training Schools, and so did the US Peace Corps volunteers. The Ford Foundation has been giving assistance in some of the projects, and in the teacher training in Indonesia as well as in the United States.

These efforts have contributed a considerable amount of materials and manpower to the improvement of teaching English in

Indonesia. On the other hand, several nonpedagogical matters seriously challenge the probability of success; for example:

1. In general, teachers are poorly paid. Therefore, many university graduates who are supposed to be English teachers switch to working in other fields which pay them much more (airlines, banks, oil companies).
2. Instructional materials are very poorly distributed and, in many areas where they already have the materials from the Ministry of Education, the teachers do not know how to use them.
3. Urbanization of English teachers. Most of the English teachers do not want to work in small towns due to the slim opportunity for moonlighting to increase their poor income, nonavailability of materials, and absence of any chance to practice and refresh their knowledge of English.

As a result, in small towns and rural areas, English is taught mostly by amateur English teachers—that is, teachers of other subjects who "know" a little English and pass it on to the students.

SOLUTION

There is a practical suggestion which is feasible, but which might raise controversy:

In the entrance examination to the high school, a language aptitude test is administered to select those who are linguistically talented and plan to continue their study at the university. Those who are selected should be given English more intensively; it is quite feasible now that the size of the English class is reduced. At any rate, for those who are not linguistically talented and do not plan to continue their study, learning English with the present system in Indonesia is only a waste of time, as it has no practical value for immediate communication and needs outside the classroom. (Controversy might arise on the question of "language talent." Some might argue that "anybody who can learn his own language normally would be able to learn any other language without much difficulty.")

LIMITED SUCCESS

Limited success in teaching English in Indonesia probably could be achieved if and when the following conditions are met:

1. When the economy of the country is much improved so that teachers are well-trained and well-paid, classroom conditions are favorable, materials are sufficient, and teacher temptation to switch to another job is reduced.
2. When motivation is increased, that is when more possibility of contact with native speakers of English and mastery of English assures a better change of earning more money.
3. When given objectives which are clearly programed in such a way as to be achievable in light of the present school circumstances (i.e., limited time allotment, oversized classes, insufficient teaching materials).
4. When the people realize that to become really educated in Indonesia, one should master an international language (i.e., English), at least at the level of reading ability, so that he can keep up with the latest developments in his field.

CONCLUSION

In Indonesia, English will never really become a strong medium of communication or enjoy the same status as in Malaysia, Singapore, and the Philippines. At most, it might become a weaker language. Some Indonesians will master the written form only (reading ability), and very few of them will be able to use it in face to face communication. This prediction is based on the following observations:

1. Indonesian is developing rapidly and is becoming a full-fledged language capable of conveying communication in the modern era.
2. There is no sense of immediate urgency for the majority of the people to learn a foreign language.
3. The needs of the majority of the population are already satisfactorily met by reading materials in Indonesian. English is needed only by highly educated persons who are compelled to master it—probably less than 1 percent of the whole population.

We think we know the roots of the problems and failures in EFL. We think we know how to solve them theoretically and we have ideas to solve them ideally. But we do not claim to be able to solve them practically, simply because many of the variables are beyond our control as individual teachers or as a group. Our motto then is, "Do what we can do and do it well." Some of the things that we can do follow.

We can make Indonesians realize the importance of English for their own careers and futures. We can show them how to study English efficiently. We can advise and train them to study by themselves and provide them with the means to achieve the goal. We can also suggest that they take a private course, as the school offering is far from sufficient. So far, the students are accustomed to being spoonfed; it is high time we made them study by themselves. Once we have done our utmost as teachers, we leave individuals to work out the problems for themselves. I believe in Darwin's law of Natural Selection, interpreted liberally. Those who want to make progress in society and realize that English is an important tool will try to do their best to improve their English. Most of these people are found in private courses all over Indonesia. It is these people who will succeed in learning English but, unfortunately, they are only a very small minority. It is these people who will become the "fittest" members of society in Darwin's "survival of the fittest."

References

1. Fishman, Joshua A. "Bilingual Sequence at the Social Level," in Kreidler (Ed.), *On Teaching English to Speakers of Other Languages*, Series II. Urbana, Illinois: National Council of Teachers of English, 1966.
2. Gregory, Dean O. *Three Projects in English Instructions in Indonesia*. Jakarta: The Ford Foundation, 1964.
3. Macnamara, John. "Problems of Bilingualism," *Journal of Social Issues*, 23 (April 1967).
4. Tan, Jan Cornelius. "English Language Teacher Training in Indonesia," unpublished dissertation, University of Michigan, 1962.
5. Weinreich, Uriel "Language in Contact," in Vol. Saporta (Ed.), Psycholinguistics. New York Holt, Rinehart and Winston, 1961.

PART TWO

Fellman's chapter should infuse optimism and hope in those concerned with the development of educational systems in newly emerging languages; it shows that achievements are possible which any prior rational appraisal would have condemned as utterly unattainable. Fellman's chapter deals with the successful reemergence of a national language which had ceased to be used in daily communication for nearly two thousand years, thus bringing to culmination the leitmotif of the three preceding chapters.

Not only had Hebrew become a so-called dead language (used even for liturgical purposes by very small numbers), but the decision to revive it was not taken by a sovereign state but, rather, by a handful of refugees who had set out to create a new future for themselves and their descendents. Yet, in less than fifty years it turned from the scantiest of beginnings—in fact one child was raised in Hebrew—into the sole medium of instruction of a fully fledged educational system comprising all levels from preschool to university. By the time independence from foreign rule was at last attained, the new medium had become so firmly entrenched that it was able to withstand the onslaught of hundreds of thousands of new non-Hebrew speaking immigrants, numbers far surpassing those of the population by which they were being absorbed.

The Teachers Did It: A Case History in the Revival of a National Language*

Jack Fellman
Bar-Ilan University
Ramat Gan, Israel

The successful revival of the Hebrew language in Israel is a unique event in sociolinguistic history, for it is the only attested case wherein a language, which had ceased to be spoken altogether for a lengthy period, was brought back into everyday spoken usage.

Hebrew is the language of one nation, the Jews. Although it closely resembles a number of Semitic languages spoken in the Near East in the second and first millennia B.C.E., it was given its characteristic form by the Israelite people in Palestine in the period between ca. 1200 B.C.E.-70 C.E. From the large amount of literature created in this language, today we possess mainly the Bible, the Dead Sea Scrolls, and the beginnings of the vast Rabbinic literature. As a result of the Roman destruction of their capital city of Jerusalem and the loss of their independence (70 C.E.), coupled with the expulsion of the Jews from large parts of Central Palestine (Judaea) after unsuccessful revolts against Roman rule (132-135 C.E.), the habit of speaking Hebrew in daily life gradually died out, and by ca. 200 C.E. it had ceased altogether.

Although it was no longer spoken, Hebrew continued to be used for reading and studying religious texts, and for thrice-daily prayers among Jews in the lands to which they had scattered, especially among those who had congregated in Near Eastern countries and in other parts of Palestine. Indeed, from ca. 900 C.E. and onward, this was the

---

*For further background, see "Israel and its People: Past and Present," by Dina Feitelson, in John Downing, *Comparative Reading*. New York: Macmillan, 1973, 426-430.

case in *all* Jewish communities, now dispersed throughout Europe, Asia, and North Africa. In several communities, Hebrew was used actively as a written language for a great variety of topics, both religious and secular. This included letters and private correspondence, business and legal documents, as well as works in the sciences and philosophy. Many Jewish communities enjoyed nearly 100 percent literacy in Hebrew among their male population, many of whom did not read or write in any other tongue.

Such a linguistic situation, wherein people are accustomed to writing in a language they do not speak and speaking in a language they do not write, in the sociolinguistic literature is called *diglossia* (6) and is considered typical of the medieval world. By contrast, the modern world is characterized by a growing sense of "linguistic nationalism" by the feeling that it is a people's right to use a single language, both in speech and in writing, as an outward symbol of collective identity.

The first person to apply the concept of linguistic nationalism to the Jewish people was a Lithuanian Jewish student, Eliezer Ben Yehuda, in an article he wrote in the Viennese Hebrew periodical *Ha-Shachar* (The Dawn) in 1879 (folio 7, pp. 3-13). The article "She'ela Nikhbada" ("A Weighty Question") posed the question of the survival of the Jews as a group with national identity vis-a-vis the assimilationist pressures of the modern, secular world. Applying the concepts of common language and common homeland to the Jews as necessary symbols for nationhood, Ben Yehuda concludes that the Jews are a nation just like all the other nations. They have a language of their own—Hebrew— and a homeland of their own—Israel. True, Hebrew is not spoken by Jews, and most Jews live outside Israel. Nevertheless, in order to ensure national continuance and achieve national revival, Jews must return to Israel and, once there, begin to speak Hebrew again.

Putting into practise what he had written, Ben Yehuda married and went to Israel in 1881, settling in Jerusalem and vowing to speak only Hebrew with the Jews with whom he would come into contact. Thus, in 1882, when his first child was born, the baby became the first child in almost two thousand years to have Hebrew as his mother tongue. Ben Yehuda hoped that, by becoming a living example of his creed, he would be able to spread his linguistic and nationalistic ideas. He further propogated his ideas through *Ha-Zevi*, a weekly newspaper which he began editing in 1884. Further, to demonstrate the adequacy of the old-new language for daily modern use, Ben Yehuda began to compile material for a dictionary which would cover the entire vocabulary of the language in all its historic periods. Whenever words to express modern concepts were lacking, Ben Yehuda did not hesitate to adapt new meanings to old forms or to coin neologisms. To help him with such lexical work, Ben Yehuda also convened a Hebrew Language Council (later to become the Hebrew Language Academy) in December 1890. [For further details on Ben Yehuda's life and work, see Fellman (*3, 4*).] However, all Ben Yehuda's efforts probably would have had *no* practical impact were it not for the fact that, six months after he arrived in Israel, a wave of violent anti-Jewish pogroms began sweeping over Eastern Europe, compelling many Jews to emigrate. Most fled westward, to Western Europe and America, but a few thousand (mainly young student-idealists) heeded the call for a return to the ancient homeland. Among these, Ben Yehuda was able to find like-minded individuals willing to test his linguistic ideas and to begin speaking Hebrew, a language familiar to them from passive use, especially from reading and from daily prayer. Ben Yehuda went even further, however, and insisted that the immigrants' children, too, immediately begin speaking Hebrew as their (near) native language. To effect this, he demanded not only that Hebrew be made a compulsory subject from the earliest grades on, but also that it be the sole language of instruction and conversation between teacher and student for *all* subjects. True, Hebrew was taught in the already existing Jewish schools in the country (most of them maintained by overseas philanthropic organizations) but only as the language of religious and classical texts. The languages of classroom instruction and conversation, however, were a variety of local languages—Arabic, Ladino, or Yiddish—as well as European tongues—French, German, or English.

What Ben Yehuda demanded seemed unreasonable and impossible, as even teachers who knew Hebrew had never before used it actively as a spoken language. While Ben Yehuda's demands had little impact on the Jews who had continued to live in the Holy Land throughout generations and those who had aggregated there over the years, the young recent arrivals were eager to start an entirely new life. Many of them were ready to entrust their children to "untrained teachers without textbooks [who] taught in an untried language, making up terminology as they went along" (*7*:2).

The problems involved in these early attempts to establish Hebrew in a budding school system can be easily imagined and, indeed, first results were far from reassuring. Most schools had no fixed curriculum and taught only two to four grades for a period of three to five years. Learning was dry and book centered, being based on repetition by rote and drilling of lists of facts, as well as literal translation of texts. Hebrew and Jewish studies dominated the classroom. The teachers themselves were mainly autodidacts without real educational experience. Hebrew still lacked necessary attributes to serve as an efficient educational tool. The most necessary terms for use in the classroom did not as yet exist in Hebrew, and there were few Hebrew textbooks. Indeed, part of each lesson was often spent in teacher dictation of facts to the pupils so that their notebooks could serve as texts. In the kindergartens and early grades, Hebrew games, songs, and dances did not yet exist. As one teacher of the period writes, "In a heavy atmosphere, without books, expressions, words, verbs, and hundreds of nouns we had to begin... teaching. It is impossible to describe or imagine under what pressure the first seeds were planted ... We were half-mute, stuttering, we spoke with our hands and eyes" (9). Similarly, another teacher of the period writes, "Every teacher had a French or Russian textbook of his own, and according to it he organized his Hebrew work.... New textbooks were not yet available... terms needed for teaching did not exist. Every village school was a world unto itself in its curriculum, teaching and coining of terms for every subject" (8:141). Gradually, however, schools were extended to include five and six grades. A Teachers Union was formed (1903), curricula began to expand, new terms were coined (especially by the Language Council with the active support of the Teachers Union), and necessary textbooks slowly began to appear. Indeed, by World War I, there were in Israel 66 all-Hebrew institutions: 20 kindergartens, 34 elementary schools (of which half had 8-year programs), 2 high schools, a women teachers' college, a kindergarten teachers' institute, two commercial schools, an art school, and an agricultural school (1:996).

Perhaps of most importance for the revival was the fact that the children who attended such schools ultimately looked upon themselves as champions of the cause of Hebrew. Even little children became staunch language patriots. For example, an extract from a 1902 newspaper, *Hashkara* (folio 17, p. 30) notes:

Here is a small and interesting story which shows that truly the children love their... language. One of the people took from a little girl who, only a month ago had begun to go to school, a doll which she held in her hand. The poor little thing, she was struck by the wicked thing he had done to her, and she grabbed the man by his coat and cried out in Hebrew: "Give it to me, give it to me!" But the man showed an indifferent face. He wanted to test the wailer; he wanted to see if she had a word in Hebrew for the noun "doll." "What should I give?" "Give it to me, give it to me!" she continued in tears, and in no way did she find a noun. But, on seeing that her robber was stubborn, she suddenly cried: "But give me... the boy of stone!" He said to her, "I don't know what that is, tell me in Yiddish and I will give you a gold coin." And in saying that, he showed her the shiny gold coin. And the girl refused, and put the gold coin in his hand and also her "boy of stone," but a non-Hebrew word she wouldn't utter under any circumstances.

The same type of steadfast loyalty to Hebrew, but on a national scale, was evident in the so-called "Language War" (3:105-110) in the years immediately preceding World War I. The German Jewish philanthropic organization, "Der Hilfsverein der deutschen Juden," had underwritten the costs of establishing a higher institute of technical learning in Haifa (later to be known as the Technion). The planners had decided that, since German was the internationally recognized language of science, it should be the language of instruction in the new institution. When this decision became widely known, demonstrations, strikes, walkouts, and protest meetings were staged by teachers, students, and parents throughout the country and the opening of the Technical High School was prevented. Most significantly, the teachers and entire student body from the Jerusalem teachers' college, which until then was run by the Hilfsverein, abandoned the premises and set up their own entirely Hebrew teachers' training institute in a private home, without any funds or backing. Similarly, in other schools throughout the country, teachers joined the revolt and started to use Hebrew for all subjects. Indeed, the language war turned into a battle against the dominance of any foreign language or culture in any Jewish school in Israel.

By the end of World War I, the battle had been won. The Technion opened with Hebrew as sole medium of instruction and plans were started for a Hebrew University, the opening of which in 1925 became a national event. In retrospect, it is clear that, more than any other factor, the introduction of Hebrew into the schools assured the ultimate success of the language revival. For, no matter what their home language(s), after several years' study in all Hebrew speaking schools, the young graduates naturally emerged with the habit of speaking Hebrew, especially to each other. Thus, when these students married among themselves, they established families and homes where Hebrew was used as a matter of course. In this way, without any further planning necessary, by the 1920s the first generation of homes had been created in which Hebrew was spoken as a matter of course. In a census taken in 1916-1917, fully 40 percent of the total Jewish population of the country (34,000 out of 85,000) declared that Hebrew was their first or daily language. Significantly, this included more than 75 percent of the children and 33 percent of the adults in the existing agricultural settlements and in the new town of Tel Aviv (2). The future of Hebrew was thus assured. The British Mandatory Administration recognized the status of Hebrew and on September 29, 1923, declared that "English, Arabic, and Hebrew shall be the official languages in Palestine." Although Hebrew was to undergo many challenges both before and after Israel achieved statehood on May 15, 1948, especially due to the several waves of immigrants which at times seemed to engulf the country, nevertheless, its status as the language of a nation living in its homeland was never in doubt—Hebrew had been revived.

References

1. Arnon, Avraham. "The History of Modern Hebrew Education in Israel," *Ha-Enziqlopedia Ha-Ivrit*, 6 (1956), 983-996 (Hebrew).
2. Bachi, Roberto. "A Statistical Analysis of the Revival of Hebrew in Israel," *Scripta Hierosolymitena*, 3 (1956), 179-247. Jerusalem: Hebrew University Press.
3. Fellman, Jack. *The Revival of a Classical Tongue: Eliezer Ben-Yehuda and the Modern Hebrew Language*. The Hague: Mouton, 1973.
4. Fellman, Jack. "The Role of Eliezer Ben-Yehuda in the Revival of the Hebrew Language," in J.A. Fishman (Ed.), *Advances in Language Planning*, 327-455. The Hague: Mouton, 1974.
5. Fellman, Jack. "The Academy of the Hebrew Language: Its History, Structure, and Function," *International Journal of the Sociology of Language*, 1 (1974), 95-103.
6. Ferguson, Charles. "Diglossia," *Word*, 15 (1959), 325-340.
7. Rabin, Chaim. "The Role of Language in Forging a Nation: The Case of Hebrew," *Incorporated Linguist*, January 1970 (five-page offprint).
8. Yellin, David. "From the Beginning Days of Creation," in David Kimhi (Ed.), *Sefer Ha-Yovel Le-Aggudat Ha-Morim* (1902-1927), 141-145, 1928 (Hebrew).
9. Yudelevitz, David. "First Reminiscences," in David Kimhi (Ed.), *Sefer Ha-Yovel Le-Aggudat Ha-Morim* (1902-1927), 150-156 (Hebrew).

PART THREE

The chapter by Mayerson and Alimi and the one by Mehrotra are further examples of the many similarities in the issues faced and the solutions attempted by educational systems in swift transition from traditional to more innovative approaches.

In both Pakistan and India, overseas experts worked with local educators in developing and disseminating a new program, in each case conceived as a comprehensive package. The work in Pakistan is still in progress; yet, despite the very recent inception of the program and the fact that it entails the acquisition of three languages by every child, one is struck by the air of quiet confidence which permeates this description, as well laid plans are being transformed step by step into instructional sequences.

Mehrotra took part in just such a process ten years earlier, when a Hindi program was being developed in India. She has stayed in close contact with the field and by now has some second thoughts. Her most serious contention is that, unduly influenced by foreign experts whose own experience was based on teaching reading in English, the team failed to make use of the specific characteristics of the Hindi writing system, and to relate suggested practices sufficiently to local conditions.

An indication that Mehrotra may be justified in her assertions can be gained from recent experience in Israel where attainments in beginning reading improved drastically in the wake of a changeover in instructional techniques (1, 2, 5). Like in Hindi, grapheme-phoneme correspondences in Hebrew are extremely consistent (3, 4).

References

1. Adiel, S. "Reading Ability of Culturally Deprived First Graders," *Megamot*, 15 (1968), 345-456 (Hebrew).
2. Adler, Ch., and R. Peleg. *Evaluating the Outcome of Studies and Experiments in Compensatory Education*. Jerusalem: Center for Research of the Disadvantaged, 1975 (Hebrew, mimeographed).
3. Feitelson, D. "Structuring the Teaching of Reading According to Major Features of the Language and Its Script," *Elementary English*, 42 (1965), 870-877.
4. Feitelson, D. "The Relationship between Systems of Writing and the Teaching of Reading," in M. Jenkinson (Ed.), *Reading Instruction: An International Forum*. Newark, Delaware: International Reading Association 1967, 191-199.
5. Feitelson, D. "Israel," in J. Downing (Ed.), *Comparative Reading*. New York: Macmillan, 1973, 426-439.

Developing a Language Curriculum in Afghanistan

Paul S. Mayerson and
M. Zaher Alimi
Ministry of Education
Kabul, Afghanistan

The study of any aspect of curriculum in Afghanistan must be viewed within a geographical and historical framework in order to better understand the problems of the development process. Knowledge of the country, and particularly its educational background, can help the reader overlay recent events upon this spatial and temporal fabric.

THE LAND AND THE PEOPLE

The Republic of Afghanistan, a Moslem nation, is a landlocked country of 250,000 square miles situated in southwestern Asia. It is characterized as a land of great geographic extremes and diversity of population and language which make curriculum building on any national scale a tenuous procedure. Afghanistan's 28 provinces contain great mountain ranges, fertile green valleys, dry barren plains, and vast deserts. The climate varies considerably from subtropical Jalalabad in the east to the year-round, snow-filled, 4,000 meter-plus Salang Pass in the Hindu Kush mountains. Temperature and rainfall vary from one part of the country to another and from one year to the next. The overall climate is hot and dry in the summer (monumental droughts occuring), with cold winters marked by snowfall in the mountains and high plateaus. Water, or the lack of it, is the key to existence in Afghanistan. The problem, historically, has not been one of sufficiency but of distribution.

About three-fourths of the estimated 19 million people are farmers who raise crops in the mountain valleys. Nomads, who roam the country with herds of livestock, make up about one-sixth of the population. Over 80 percent of the people speak one or both of the two official languages, Dari (Afghan Persian) and Pashto, both Indo-European in origin. In addition, over twenty other dialects and regional languages are spoken in various parts of the country.

Although education in Afghanistan is free and the law states that all children between the ages of seven and thirteen should attend elementary school, fewer than 50 percent were enrolled previously. For those few who managed to complete the first six grades, secondary schools, Kabul University, and some other institutions of higher education were available. Most elementary school leavers, however, have not reached the sixth grade and have tended to remain in their local areas, following the customs, language, and occupations of their families and generally losing whatever they had acquired of the ability to read and write.

This has led, generally, to a multilingual, nonliterate, nonmobile, inward-looking society engaged in basic food production, extracting a marginal living under difficult circumstances, and intent on perpetuating the status quo—not the most promising conditions for curriculum or any other kind of innovation.

THE DEVELOPMENT OF EDUCATION

When viewing the development of education from an historical perspective, several main phases can be identified, often overlapping and still coexisting today.

The first phase is the traditional type of education, dating from the introduction of Islamic culture to the world over 1,200 years ago, and carried on in the home, the mosque, and the madrassah (school). Traditional forms stressed religious education through the teaching of the Holy Koran, reading, writing, some elementary arithmetic skills, and moral instruction on the responsibilities of the individual to society at large. In addition, the child was prepared for an occupation, such as reading the Holy Koran and calligraphy or letter writing. Traditional education taught the student to become a good Muslim and a contributing member to a traditional society. One may say that the objectives were essentially religious and moral.

So-called modern education was introduced at the beginning of the 20th century with the creation of regular primary and secondary schools and the establishment of the forerunner of the present Ministry of Education. Grades, examinations, and disciplinary regulations were set on western models while curricula were prepared with attention given to national needs and tendencies. The general objectives of this period of development were to prepare a relatively small number of students to be literate and enter the secondary school in order to become the administrative personnel required for the creation and perpetuation of a modern state.

Textbooks were written in the two mother tongues—Persian and Pashto—and, in addition, lessons were taught in theology, the Holy Koran, Tafseer (commentaries on the Holy Koran), arithmetic, some geometry, and calligraphy. Teaching materials for calligraphy (wooden board, white chalk, reed pen, paper, and locally made black ink) are still in general use today, although the ballpoint pen has begun to make its mark. The natural and social sciences were gradually added to the curriculum during the middle of this period. In the thirties, forties, and fifties, changing conditions mandated revisions in the curricula and texts at all levels of education. Many books printed during this period are still in use.

The beginning of the third phase coincides with the first of the five-year plans (1957-1962) which stressed the increase of primary education and literacy for all of society's members in order to implement reforms in sanitation, agriculture, commerce, construction, and industry. The acceptance of planning as an approach in the process of accelerating development and the awareness of the essential role that education had to play in that process truly mark the beginning of "modern" education. By the end of the second five-year plan, a national commission had formulated the goals and objectives which have governed the preparation of instructional materials since that time.

The fourth phase of historical development must date from the creation of the Republic of Afghanistan on July 17, 1973 under the leadership of President Mohammad Daud, and the subsequent publication of the Educational Reform document detailing the philosophical directions for education in the future. These directions are stated in the first paragraph of that document, as follows:

To bring into existence a modern educational system in accordance with the needs of the time and reflect the aspirations of today's society is a top objective of our young Republican State. Today's society expects the educational system to be a torch to enlighten children in the best way, to be a useful means of strengthening and training the mental, physical, and psychological abilities of our youth. Our educational system must be structured in such a way as to really elevate the educational standard of the children of the country, to be effective in the formation of a healthy society consisting of philanthropic and patriotic individuals observing Islamic principles and civil laws of the country and believing in traditions and historical values of the country, and to be able to spread knowledge through the people with such characteristics.

THE PROCESS OF CURRICULUM DEVELOPMENT

The development of curricula and instructional materials is a continuous process. Changes are necessary because of new knowledge and skills technology constantly being discovered in all subject areas and because of new methods discovered in teaching and learning of these subjects. Also, social, economic, and political developments demand that changes be made.

Curriculum development in the Afghan Ministry of Education can be described in an eight phase process. Briefly stated, these phases are as follows:

1. Educational goals are stated.
2. Scope and sequence are developed.
3. Manuscripts are written.
4. Trial materials are approved.
5. Field trials are conducted and evaluated.
6. Materials are revised, approved, and printed.
7. Supervisors and teachers are oriented to the texts.
8. Texts are evaluated in view of future revision.

Goals and Objectives

Educational goals based on national goals and objectives of the Educational Reform of January 1975 are stated and then used as a guide to transform them into an approved curriculum. The curriculum, in turn, provides an outline to guide the creation and production of instructional materials (pupils' books and teachers' guides for each grade level, a scope and sequence).

At the time of the Republican Revolution on July 17, 1973, all previous statements of goals and objectives were reviewed and instructional materials were revised accordingly. This led eventually to the Educational Reform document when curricula and materials were reinterpreted in terms of stated objectives.

In 1966, during the second five-year plan, a Curriculum and Textbook Project was established (under the Elementary Education Department of the Ministry of Education) for the express purpose of developing curricula and their necessary instructional materials. (In 1973, the project was made a part of the Publications Department which historically has had the responsibility for preparing new textbooks.) Technical assistance for this project has been provided by Teachers College, Columbia University, New York, under a contract with the United States Agency for International Development.

Writing sections were organized within the Curriculum and Textbook Project, corresponding to each subject in the elementary school course of study. One of the largest sections was and is the Language Arts Section which consists of 28 members—including one foreign advisor—preparing a total of 64 texts and teachers' guides for grades one through eight. The section is organized into five divisions: Dari and Pashto as mother tongues (first language), Dari for Pashto speakers and Pashto for Dari speakers (second language), and English (foreign language).

Each division within the Language Arts Section has had the responsibility of developing a curriculum within its own sphere of operation.

The Scope and Sequence

A sequential program for the introduction of concepts, knowledge, and skills is developed for each grade level, based on the curriculum plan developed in the first phase of the process.

The language arts program is of fundamental importance to the elementary school curriculum. Since all books in all subjects are written in both Dari and Pashto, the two official languages, language arts learnings contribute to learning effectiveness in other subject areas. Therefore, the scope and sequence in language arts must become an integrated statement of the total language experience of children in school.

Since each of the two languages is the mother tongue for some children and a second language for others, the language arts program is initially divided into these two major parts: teaching of mother tongue (first language) and teaching of second language. Whether a school is situated in a predominantly Dari speaking or Pashto speaking region determines which language is considered the first language and which the second.

Teaching of the mother tongue begins in the first grade and continues throughout the child's school career. The new materials and methods have attempted to integrate the major communication skills into a coordinated series of learning experiences directed towards the development of thinking, reasoning, and creative abilities.

Second language teaching, beginning at the fourth grade, and foreign language teaching (English), introduced at the sixth grade level, emphasize the importance of communicating with Afghans in other sections of the country and with the outside world.

Emphasis in all three programs is placed on situations and topics that are immediate and relevant to the child's everyday life. The scope and sequence for grades one to three includes concepts from social studies, health, science, and practical works, presented in a series of related activities and skills. A curriculum based on the "world of work," developed for the upper classes, provides children with sufficient information to better understand their relationships to their environments. The activities, skills, and learnings introduced in each language program meet its unique needs as well as meeting the needs of one of the other language programs. (This is described more fully in the section on the "Integration of Activities.")

The Preparation of Manuscripts

The scope and sequence developed in the second phase of the development process is used to design basic research and to create manuscripts for pupils' texts and teachers' guides which will be tried out experimentally in the schools.

Traditional teaching. Previously, elementary textbooks were written by individuals without direct reference to the learners who had to use them or the teachers who had to teach them. There were few teaching instructions available.

The traditional techniques of language teaching were essentially as follows. First, pupils were taught the Dari or Pashto alphabet, an expanded Arabic script. Attention then turned to reading and writing. Reading methods consisted of the teacher's reading aloud a sentence or page to the pupils. Next, the pupils repeated the sentence or page along with the teacher, and then they chanted the words in unison

　　　　　　　　　　　　　　　　MAYERSON AND ALIMI

without the teacher. This process was repeated over and over. Finally, the teacher chose a page from the now memorized material and asked a child to read it. If the child had been an attentive pupil, he could "read" the page without looking at the written symbols. The teacher then chose another successful pupil to lead the chant and this was continued page by page, day by day until some children memorized each page. Reading became simply parroting for memorization.

The old methods made no attempt to guide vocabulary development nor was there any established sequence of skills for the language arts, which meant that there was little attempt to teach the basic structure of the language.

Writing was treated as a separate subject—calligraphy. Letters, nonsense syllables, words, and sentences—not necessarily correlated with the reading material—were written on the chalkboard or in printed exercise books, and then copied over and over by the pupils. Much more attention was paid to proper letter formation in relation to the model given, than to the usefulness of the written language as a means of communicating ideas. There was little or no direction for developing creative composition; in fact, the basic organizational skills necessary to develop the logical exposition of an idea were not taught.

Little attention was devoted to the skills of speaking and listening except as they related to memorization and recitation. There was no planned activity for creative expression and little was done to help the child in conceptual development.

The New Approach. The usual procedure now in preparing textbooks for language arts is that two or three members of the Language Arts Section in each official language are identified to be responsible for preparation of all relevant materials at a particular grade level. Before attempting to translate the scope and sequence into a table of contents, required baseline research is conducted to try to determine a suitable point of departure.

To give one example germane to the development of the first three texts, in-depth studies were made of children's vocabulary in the two official languages to determine the most commonly used words. These word studies were used to introduce children to a controlled vocabulary. The purpose was to use the most common words in Dari or Pashto in a repetitive pattern during exercises in speaking, listening, reading, and writing in order to promote a complete understanding of these words in a variety of contexts. These words then served as a foundation upon which to build the children's language skills.

Following the research phase, the two language groups merge in order to plan a common series of experiences for all Afghan children, no matter in which language they are receiving instruction. Later, when writing, the authors create their own stories and skills which grow out of and are unique to their own native language, in order to preserve its flavor, rhythm, and structure.

The Components of the Program. The language arts program, as developed for the elementary schools, has three major components; the reading materials, the skills activities, and an accompanying teacher's guide. In the first few weeks of the first grade, readiness books with some charts and teacher's instructions are used, but after this initial period, the first reader (with charts), an accompanying skills text, and their teacher's guide are introduced. The second and third grades follow the same pattern. All components for each grade are integrated into one teacher's guide.

In the fourth through eighth grades for all programs (i.e. first, second, and foreign language), the pupils' reading materials and skills activities are incorporated into one book with the usual accompanying guide.

Each text contains stories, essays, playlets, riddles, and poems of people, places, and events designed to foster an appreciation of the uniqueness and versatility of Afghan culture. For first language instruction in the first three grades, each book is organized into twenty stories and four poems. These have been selected with reference to the child's needs and interests within the culture in a progression from the simple to the more difficult.

In grades four through eight the text is organized into five units, each with five stories and a poem built around major topics so that each can be explored in greater depth and with a variety of approaches. The topics and skills of each unit are varied enough to provide broad coverage, although some are inevitably repeated in other books of the series with different focus.

Whereas the curriculum in grades one through three centers around the child and moves outward concentrically as his horizons broaden, the curriculum in grades four through eight is designed to impart knowledge and skills of a useful and productive nature drawn from the world of work as mandated by the Educational Reform. In both the five year second language sequence and the three year foreign language program, each book features thirty lessons with topics drawn to meet the same objectives of immediacy, relevancy, and appropriateness in terms of Afghan culture.

The New Methodology: First Language. In studying the mother tongue, pupils begin in the first grade with readiness activities designed to assure that they are physically and psychologically mature enough to recognize and write language symbols. They are then introduced to written words which are easily understood because they are a part of their spoken vocabulary. These words are introduced gradually so that there is considerable practice in different contexts. First, they are made into sentences and then into short stories so that the children learn to read them in context and to recognize them individually. They are asked to use the new words orally and to write them in short sentence/stories reflecting their own experiences.

Much interaction takes place between the pupils and the teacher, with both actively involved in each lesson through discussion questions exploring ideas and concepts related to the stories presented. A good balance is kept between oral and silent reading with pupils encouraged to find answers to questions posed. The mechanical chanting of the past has no place in the new program.

Thus, in the new approach, children learn to use word symbols as tools for expressing their own ideas, both orally and in writing, in ways which can be understood by those with whom they wish to communicate.

The New Methodology: Second Language. Teaching a second language, introduced in the fourth grade, requires use of methods which are different from those used in teaching a first language (although, previously, the only method used was the usual rote-memorization of pages described earlier). In the first language, children have a spoken vocabulary when they begin school. They have already associated sound symbols with things and experiences in their everyday lives. Learning a second language means associating new sounds with familiar objects, activities, and ideas.

Thus, the first step in teaching a second language involves building a new spoken vocabulary in which unfamiliar sounds are related to familiar experiences. These are then gradually integrated into the structure of the new language which differs from the native language. The teacher's guide for second language teaching is carefully constructed to show teachers, step by step, how to go about this procedure.

Pupils are encouraged to speak and listen in the second language. As they grow in proficiency, they are progressively introduced to related reading and writing learning activities. Gradually, more and more first language teaching methods can be used.

The New Methodology: Foreign Language. The Educational Reform stipulates that, beginning in the sixth grade (rather than the seventh as was done in the past), all children are to be introduced to a foreign language. For the vast majority, the foreign language will be English.

Learning a foreign language is different from learning the mother tongue or the second language. A distinctively new set of sound and written symbols must be learned, which is further complicated in an Afghan setting in that a complete change of direction is also required—that of going from left to right rather than from right to left. All the required activities and methods were previously introduced in the basic English course, but through the attrition of time, present practice has reverted to the same methodology already described in first and second language.

The three year sequence of English language instructions (grades six through eight) is designed to lay a foundation of skills and understandings which can serve as a starting point in developing a means of communication with the rest of the world. For Afghan children, this will mean an emphasis on reading and writing skills, along with those of listening and speaking, from the very first lesson.

In the beginning, stress is placed on utilising situations that are immediate and relevant to everyday life. To the extent that time will allow, topics will reflect the socially, culturally, and economically oriented aims of the Educational Reform.

Teachers' guides for English are written in three languages. The introduction, which contains a detailed step by step approach to all teaching procedures, is written in Dari and Pashto on opposite pages. The day by day structured lesson plans are written in English, which will remind the teachers to teach in English and, incidentally, help their own English competency.

The Integration of Activities. Activities for all language arts textbooks serve two purposes. First, they are designed to meet the unique needs of learning and communicating in the mother tongue, second, or foreign language. Second, they are meant to complement those activities, skills, and learnings which are introduced in one of the other language programs. Although some overlap is inevitable, the plan generally is to try not to duplicate the teaching of a particular skill. It may be practiced and reinforced, but not introduced as a major unit of work.

One example would be dramatization. This is introduced as a suggested activity in the first three grades. During the intermediate grades, the emphasis on direct communication and expression is shifted to the second language program through the use of social conversation and situational dialogues. Because of the decrease of timetable allotments for first language, it was felt that other, more important skills should be emphasized. Subsequently, this is shifted to the foreign language program, which encourages the use of dramatic situations, and eventually back to first language by including short plays as part of the reading materials in grades seven and eight.

Another example of interrelatedness would be the inclusion of word building activities in the middle grades' first language program. An analysis of both programs turns up examples of work with synonyms, antonyms, suffixes, and prefixes which are borrowed from the other official language in the form of cognates which help in building the awareness of borrowed vocabulary.

The Work Cycle of Activities. Perhaps the major form of integration and revolutionary departure from the normal is the design of the teaching unit and the teacher's guide. Recognizing that many of this generation of teachers in Afghanistan come to the classroom with limited training and background, it was decided at the outset that all teaching instruction, at this stage of textbook development, would be highly structured in order to provide the teacher with a maximum of matter and method to instill greater confidence and to lead to a higher degree of competence.

This has been accomplished through the utilisation of a set work cycle of activities in each text. In the first three grades, a seven day cycle of reading and language development activities was chosen to maximize the learning of the skill strands. The magic number of seven was determined after experimentation with eight and nine day cycles. The seven day cycle for grades one to three is as follows.

The first day includes introducing and reading the story, a word study segment, an interpretation activity, and a workbook activity in the language skills worktext. Days two to six involve rereading the story in one or another form, more word study, a section based on one of the related areas such as science, and another worktext activity. Day seven requires rereading the story for the final time, a word study activity, and a creative writing assignment taken from the worktext. The cycle of worktext activities generally includes handwriting, language usage, study skills, related subject activities, poetry, vocabulary building, and creative writing.

In grades four through eight, a six day cycle was chosen to correspond to the six timetabled recitations per week. The activities include reading and rereading the story; comprehension, interpretation, and other study skills; vocabulary building skills; a language development strand; and a composition and creative writing day.

The second language program is based on a five day cycle with each day given over to stressing one of the four communication skills and a fifth day devoted to a review of the week's work and a quiz. Within any one day, all four skills are practiced with emphasis on one as mentioned. Foreign language teaching makes use of a three day cycle which concentrates on practicing each of the four skills during the 35-40 minutes alloted on the timetable.

The importance of these preselected sets of skills and exercises is that it allows the teacher to perfect his/her teaching approach over a four or five week period through repetition of a particular kind of activity. Activities are changed frequently enough to avoid boredom on the part of the teacher and the learner, but the emphasis on a particular skill strand on a certain day throughout the school year reinforces confidence in changed subject matter.

Two byproducts of this stringent structuring have become apparent over the years. First, and most important, has been the development of an ever increasing corps of Afghan teachers who are becoming aware of the teaching/learning process, in addition to building competence in handling specific classroom situations.

Second has been the building of skilled Afghan writers of language arts texts and teaching materials who are also becoming knowledgeable about the psychology of language learning. They have also developed a commonality of vocabulary which permits the writer of the second grade Pashto skills activities to communicate on a professional level with the writer of the sixth grade Dari reader. This means that members of the Language Section are able to seek each other's advice in order to provide the flexibility necssary to cope with their task.

MAYERSON AND ALIMI

The Approval of Materials

As texts are written, they are discussed with senior editors and advisors, both in and out of the section. The texts then are revised on the basis of these discussions before submitting them for review and approval.

The review and approval stage is accomplished by the Ministry of Education through its appointed agent, the review committee. The review committee is composed of personnel drawn from within the section, the Publications Department, the Ministry of Education at large, and other educators from the university and teacher training institutions. They are charged with the responsibility of reviewing the manuscripts and making recomendations on their suitability as trial materials in the schools selected for field tryouts. Judgments are made concerning authenticity, relevance to Afghan cultural values, validity of content and method, and, most importantly, "the proper use of language."

The Field Tryout Period

Field trials of approved manuscripts are conducted in laboratory and other cooperating schools. Research is conducted to determine the effectiveness of the materials; this serves as a basis for revising and remitting to the Ministry of Education for final approval to print.

Historically, books were written for children without reference to whether children could learn from them. Little attention was given to the modern educational principles which underlie the teaching/learning process. Now, after a text has been approved by the review committee, a full academic year is usually devoted to its trial use to determine its validity.

Trial schools are selected from ordinary schools, designated cooperating schools, and laboratory schools. Both experimental and control populations are established before the newly written trial materials are distributed in limited numbers. (Attempts are also made to see that the control population has access to traditional materials.) Teachers who will teach the trial materials are oriented to their use by members of the Language Section and asked to proceed with the trial under as close to normal classroom conditions as possible.

Periodic observation and supervisory visits are made by the authors and other Ministry of Education personnel to ensure that the materials are being used as planned and to make on-the-spot judgments for any necessary immediate alterations. After use for one or two terms, the children's achievement is tested for both the control and experimental populations and assessed in light of the major objective of "How effective are the new materials as opposed to the traditional materials?" Subjective judgments of teachers, pupils, headmasters, and supervisors are also collected and analyzed. The sum total of all data is evaluated and recommendations for revision are made in committee.

Materials are then prepared in their final form and sent back to the Ministry of Education for final approval.

Printing and Distributing the Materials

After receiving final approval, the materials are made ready to be sent to the press for publication. Printing specifications are determined and calculations are made as to the quantity to print using data supplied by the Department of Planning and the Book Distribution Center. It has been the practice to print a two or three year supply of each text, depending on the policy of repeated usage for any grade level.

In cooperation with the Language Section, the press officials monitor the printing schedule and supervise the conformity of the book with the accepted printing specifications. In the matter of specifications, the language arts texts have required several unique decisions. First of all has been the matter of type size. Since no research exists for children's reading in Arabic script, the decision was made to begin with 36 point type and gradually reduce the type size in subsequent grades until 14 point was reached by the sixth grade. Various leadings were adopted to accommodate the supposed increased visual acuity of more mature children.

A second area of concern has been the choice of type style. Hand written Dari is usually in Nastaliq style, a form of cursive handwriting common in the literature and the sign of one who is literate in Persian. There is no type case available in Nastaliq, which means that any work in this style must be hand calligraphed and then printed photo offset. Usually, printing in Persian is done in Naskh style for which a type case exists. Pashto is also printed and written in Naskh. The decision was made to print all language arts texts in Naskh except where exact models were required in order to teach handwriting and these would be hand calligraphed and printed photo offset.

A third determination to be made on specifications concerned direction in terms of either a textbook or a worktext approach. Ministry of Education policy has been that books written for the first three grades are to be used for one year and then become the property of the user. This, however, can be a very expensive undertaking, especially considering the large size format of worktext materials which must accommodate the large handwriting models for reed pen users. A recent change in policy has indicated that textbooks in the first two grades will have a life expectancy of two years. This has solved the financial problem but not the textbook versus the worktext problem as it also has been policy that children write in the worktexts. These have already been printed in several years' supply. The problem remains to be resolved.

Last has been the matter of textbook illustration. Although there are artists in Afghanistan, few have been trained in the art of book illustration. Therefore, it has been difficult to maintain consistency from page to page and from book to book within a series. Model pictures have now been established for all family members and a very rigorous review of art work is imposed to ensure authenticity and conformity to Afghan culture.

On completion of printing and binding, sufficient copies of the books are reserved for advance usage in teacher education activities, for the use of the section, and for other educational purposes. The press then notifies the Book Distribution Center that the books are ready for delivery and distribution to the provinces.

The Orientation of Teachers

Administrators, supervisors, and teachers are oriented and trained to use the new materials properly. The present method is carried out on a regional basis as follows:

Before a full workshop for any group is scheduled, a small team from the Materials Orientation Section and Research Section of the Department of Publications visits a regional center for two purposes. The first is to arrange with governors of several provinces to hold a seminar for administrators, supervisors, and inspectors at some date in the near future. The second is to visit selected schools for a preseminar observation of classroom teaching without benefit of orientation. (This is followed up after the seminar and is described in the next phase below.)

At the agreed upon date, a staff made up of experienced members of the writing sections and others from the Department of Publications hold a seminar for all those in the region responsible for overseeing and supervising materials being used in the classroom. They are oriented and taught how to teach the new methods for all textbooks at a particular grade level. Following an intensive period of work, including practice teaching, the trainees hold a seminar for teachers in the provincial center under the watchful eyes of the team from the Department of Publications who criticizes their performance at the end of each session. After returning to their home areas, the now newly qualified teacher-trainers replicate the seminar experience for more groups of teachers until almost all in any province have been oriented. To date, there have been eight such seminars with the remainder planned so that the entire country will eventually be exposed to the newer approaches.

Evaluation and Revision

The teachers use the new materials in the schools and with the children. Objective and subjective data are collected from the field to determine the materials' effectiveness and usefulness in meeting the objectives stated in the first phase of the development process.

Curriculum development is a continuous process. Included in the procedures for development is the collection of data on the use of the new teachers' guides and pupils' books with a view to revising the material in the future. Such revision is necessary due to the need to include new information as, knowledge increases; to correct deficiencies which show up as the material comes into national use; and to reflect political, social, and economic changes which develop as the Republic succeeds in becoming a modern democratic state responsive to the needs of the people.

To aid in this aim, after a reasonable amount of time, a follow-up team from the Department of Publications visits a region where orientation seminars have been given. This team spot-checks distribution of the textbooks to schools and utilization of the materials in the classroom. Upon their return to the Ministry of Education, they report to the appropriate authorities and to the section which begins the process over again to prepare the second edition.

SUMMARY

The Ministry of Education in Afghanistan is modernizing the national elementary school curriculum through the systematic development of new syllabi and the preparation of instructional materials.

The traditional curriculum emphasizes rote memorization of excessively academic materials, detached from the realities of family, community, and national life. The new approach encourages active inquiry, problem solving, and an exploration of ideas and concepts germane to a modern society.

The new language arts program is of fundamental importance to the new primary curriculum.

Teaching of the children's mother tongue begins in their first year of school. The new methods and materials integrate the major communication skills and direct them toward the development of thinking, reasoning, and creative abilities.

Children's second language development is begun in the fourth grade to help people of various language groups in Afghanistan to better understand one another.

Sixth grade children begin a sequence of foreign language teaching which serves as a starting point in developing a means of communication with the rest of the world.

Emphasis in all three programs is placed on situations and topics that reflect the child's everyday life. The scope and sequence for the first three grades also includes concepts from social studies, health, science, and practical works which are presented in a series of related activities and skills. The upper class currriculum is based on the world of work and helps provide children with information to better understand their relationships to their environments.

The activities, skills, and learnings introduced in each language program meet the unique needs of that language. Second, they complement those which are introduced in another program.

For the first time in Afghanistan, teachers' guides have been prepared. Each is carefully constructed to show teachers, step-by-step, how to meet the challenges of teaching the new materials.

The new language arts materials for Afghan elementary schools provide learning experiences designed to assist pupils in building better lives for themselves and their families and contributing to the progress of their communities and country.

Issues in Developing Materials for Beginning Reading in Hindi*

Preet Vanti Mehrotra
University of Delhi
Delhi, India

Hindi is the acclaimed official language of the Republic of India. Hindi is expected to replace English for the purpose of interstate communication very soon. But Hindi is not the mother tongue of all Indians. Schedule VIII of our Constitution lists as many as fifteen languages which are recognized as national languages of our country. Hindi is only one of them and fresh additions to this list are in the offing.

In the world of education, the geographical, cultural, and multilingual conditions of our people have given rise to the Three-Language Formula. Accordingly, every child is expected to have his mother tongue as the medium of instruction at the primary level and to learn two other languages (English and Hindi or another regional language). Individual states are free to accommodate the three languages within their school curriculum according to their conditions. No wonder that instruction in Hindi does not start at any specified age uniformly over the country. It is introduced in the first grade in the Hindi speaking states and in the third, fifth, sixth or eighth grade in the non-Hindi speaking ones. Moreover, "beginners" in Hindi can be found often among adults working in government offices and institutions. Evidently, issues involved in developing materials for beginning reading in Hindi would differ according to the varying nature of the beginners—their first language, age, experience, and

---

*For further background, see "India," by Chinna Oommen, in John Downing, *Comparative Reading*. New York: Macmillan, 1973, 403-425.

needs. That reading materials in Hindi must be selected, graded, and organised with such important factors in mind as the age, ability, interests, experiences, and needs of the various categories of beginners is an obvious and endless issue. I would not dare to touch upon its intricacies. I would rather limit my discussion to the issues involved in developing materials for beginning reading in Hindi as the mother tongue.

For centuries, Hindi has been taught and learned in its various forms—spoken and written, standard and dialectal—by millions of pupils in or out of school. Individual writers and publishers have been engaged in the task of printing primers for beginners, logically presenting all the letters of the alphabet with pictures and words. Identification of single letters, memorisation of letter sequences, learning simple words formed from combinations of vowels and consonants have been the first essential steps toward learning reading. Reading groups of words forming separate sentences and reading sequences of sentences forming paragraphs have been used invariably as subsequent steps to practicing and reinforcing reading skills. Parents, teachers, and literate adults with Hindi as their mother tongue have all learned reading through such alphabetic primers.

More than ten years ago, as part of the Reading Project Team of the National Council of Educational Research and Training, I shared the pleasure and pains of preparing a new type of initial reading material for Hindi speaking children. Under the guidance of experts from abroad, the team discussed, deliberated, and decided upon a course of action which was enthusiastically and rigorously translated into reality. Children's spoken vocabulary was surveyed. A Reading Readiness Kit and a Reading Primer were prepared within record time. An exhaustive volume containing elaborate guidelines for the preparation and production of textbooks in the mother tongue was brought out. In due course, a set of five graded readers in Hindi was prepared to follow the Primer. The Primer, as well as each reader, was accompanied by a teachers' manual and a pupils' workbook. Millions of these pupils' books and thousands of teachers' manuals have been printed and used since then. Seminars and workshops have been organised, and demonstration lessons and training and supervision work have been done by members of the Project Team. After initial tryout, the Primer and other basal readers have been prescribed not only in Delhi schools but in some other Hindi speaking states, also.

How the initial reading materials were produced, received, and used brings out the issues involved in such a task. Surveys of children's, teachers' and parents' reactions have been made periodically. Strong and weak points of the approach have been discussed and identified. Modifications in the approach and materials have been devised and are in process.

MAJOR ISSUES FACED IN PREPARING THE PRIMER

1. Which "approach" to adopt—traditional (alphabetic or phonic) or progressive (look-and-say)?
2. Which form of language to include—spoken or literary?
3. Which words to include—without mātrās (vowel symbols) with mātrās, or both?
4. Which forms of Hindi words and grammatical structures to adopt out of the many familiar forms?

(आ, आओ, आइए) (खा, खाओ, खाइए)
(भाई, भैया, भाईसाहब) (मां, अम्मा, माताजी)
(बापू, बाबा, बाबू, पिताजी)

(aa, aao, aiyé) (khaa, khaao, khaiyé)
(bhai, bhaiya, bhai, saheb) (maan, amma, mataji)
(baapu, baba, babu, pitaji)

5. Which spellings to choose out of several acceptable forms ?

(भइया, भैया) (खाइर, खाइये)
(bhaiya) (khaiyé)

6. Which form of sociocultural setting to present—high, middle, or low? Rural or urban?
7. Which format to adopt—formal reading lessons or picture pages with conversational captions?
8. Which form of organisation to adopt—a set of connected episodes around the same characters or a few unrelated themes?
9. How to reach the teacher—through a detailed teachers' guide book or short hints included in the pupils book?

In finding solutions for the above issues, broad objectives of universal education in a socialistic democratic country were taken into account. Innovative practices in preparing initial reading materials current in the West were studied diligently. Learning theories and psychological findings in the context of learning to read English meaningfully, easily, and interestedly were given primary importance. The economic aspect of production and consumption were tackled properly. The result was an attractive, 75 paise Primer (78 pages long) full of lovely, thought provoking illustrations, introducing some 48 Hindi words of high frequency in the spoken vocabulary of six-year-olds. It was organized in the form of original anecdotes woven around three children in a middle-class Indian family with moderately educated loving parents speaking standard Hindi (Khari Boli), in a realistic setting. Desirable habits of work and play, keen curiosity and affection, happy attitudes and spontaneous discipline were presented in an interesting manner. Intimate, respectful verb forms were adopted rather than the crude root forms found mostly in primers.

(jao, jaā) (utho, uth) (khao, khaā)

Suspense and surprise, fun and humour, and love for animals and birds found full play in the course of three units comprising the text. An average Hindi speaking child's environment and experiences were tapped artistically. Sufficient scope for the beginner's guessing, thinking, and imagining was left by discreetly controlling and arranging page to page. Short, simple, and familiar words were incorporated in short, natural utterances and repeated religiously through the following pages. No artificial barrier was created between words with mātrās and without.

(रानी, मदन, अमर, मां, पिताजी)

(Rani, Madan, Amar, Maan, Pilji)

Even compound words were included

(बन्दरवाला, भालूवाला, फलवाला)

(Bandarwala, Bhaluwala, Phalwala)

smoothly. In spelling, the simpler version

(मैया, कौवा)

(Bhaiya, Kauwa)

was adopted. Exercises in word analysis, word building, and comprehension were set after each unit. However, the main intention and emphasis was on building a limited sight vocabulary. That is why the whole text covered only sixteen consonants and six vowel symbols. To go with the primer, an elaborate teachers' manual was produced (120 pages long) explaining why and how to go about the task of introducing the six-year-olds to reading Hindi through the newly-devised primer. Sets of flash cards, letter cards, charts, and wall pictures were made available to go with the text.

More than ten years of experience with newly devised initial reading materials in Hindi have revealed that a well-illustrated, properly set story primer appeals immediately to the young beginners. The younger the beginner, the more he likes such a book in comparison with the formal conventional primers presenting logically sequenced letters of the alphabet with tiny illustrations and lots of phonic drills and word combination exercises. Moreover, it requires a whole team of dedicated workers to bring out a set of reading materials—research workers, writers, teachers, reviewers, illustrators, producers, and printers. To keep the quality of production high and the price of books low, nationalised, subsidised books are, perhaps, the only answer.

However, the practical, teaching value of a picture primer in Hindi, with major emphasis on a limited sight vocabulary, is very restricted indeed. Its content coverage is little and it ignores three major factors: 1) the nature of the beginner, 2) the nature of the Hindi language, and 3) the psychology of the teacher.

The assumption underlying the reading materials provided in "Rani, Madan, Amar" that the first grade entrant would be about six-years-old and would be absolutely ignorant about the Hindi writing system is open to question. The assumption may be true of many children, but there is a class of preprimary children from educated homes who have already had their elementary lessons in reading Hindi. They enter grade one with a familiarity with letter names and letter shapes in their logical sequence. They can decode simple words without, or even with, mātrās. Such children may be already well set on their path to reading Hindi. Then, there is a class of children (a more numerous group) coming from poorer backgrounds who are older in age than the normal six years, but who have had no experience in reading and no instruction in the alphabet. They seldom have been exposed to the written word, but their spoken vocabulary and maturity levels are usually far above those of six-year-olds. Their understanding, awareness, power of logical thinking, discrimination, and interpretation are naturally of a higher level.

The varied nature of reading readiness found among primary school entrants is a challenge too hard to be met by a single set of reading materials. Another assumption held in devising the new materials, which is open to challenge, is about the nature of the Hindi language. Unlike English, the writing system of Hindi is found to be consistent and smooth. Learning the alphabet names and shapes before launching on reading words and sentences is helpful to the beginner. Since there is no phoneme-grapheme confusion in the Hindi writing system, a child can decode any text once he learns the vowel and consonant letters and how they combine. The sight-vocabulary approach makes learning to read Hindi unnecessarily complicated, difficult, and long for both pupil and teacher. To prefer the look-and-say approach to the alphabetic approach in Hindi seems to be preferring conditioning to logical thinking.

Another aspect of the nature of Hindi which does not correspond with the expectations of a perfect experience approach is its infinite variety. There are hundreds of dialectal variations within the Hindi Language and there are dozens of variants within the Khari Boli. The vocabulary, word forms, and grammatical patterns observed in the book are not every Hindi speaking child's heritage. Ways of addressing members in a social group, marks of respect, intimacy and affection, forms of adjectives and verbs, vary from group to group and family to family. No single uniform set of standard Hindi reading materials can satisfy the demands and realities of an experience approach for beginning to read Hindi. There is every chance of "misreading" the presented text if the beginner is guided into reading on the basis of his own experience. An initial familiarity with the grapheme-phoneme patterns would certainly save a beginner from such pitfalls as reading

(बाबूजी for पिताजी, on खाले for खाओ, or दादा for भैया)

(Babuji for Pilaji, or, Kha lé for Khao or Dada for Bhaiya).

Another category of facts, not considered very seriously, concerns the teacher of Hindi. The teacher who initiates a class of fifty or more children has his/her limitations. Under special pressure, the teacher may go through the details of the teachers' manual, but may not be able to translate the suggestions into reality. The large number of children and the variations in their reading readiness levels stand as stumblingblocks to the smooth dialogue expected for fixing the imagination, stirring the experience, and motivating the child. Under normal conditions, the Hindi teacher is reluctant to teach the way our progressive approach demands. Why? Because, in the context of the composition of the class, it is slow, cumbersome, arduous, and uneconomical.

The conventional approach to beginning reading in Hindi has been the alphabetic one, a logical approach, moving from simple to complex, from short to long, from elements to compounds. No doubt there is room for modification in this approach, but it doesn't seem necessary or desirable to give it up altogether. If utility, frequency, and productivity are kept in mind while introducing letters as well as words in beginners' reading materials, and if we devise interesting and meaningful reading materials for readers, why should the beginners not learn reading? Why should they not love reading? Why should they not continue reading? One learns reading by reading, not talking. One learns reading fast by practicing fast reading of interesting, useful, and extensive materials, not by reading a few words slowly and repeatedly. "There is no reading problem," says John Kolt. "There are problem teachers and problem schools." To my mind, we need to carry out much more vigorous grass roots research on native soil before we can agree or disagree with an emphatic assertion like this in the context of Hindi. However, I do believe Kolt is absolutely right when he says it helps to build from everyday experience rather than from a textbook.

PART FOUR

The chapters by Kim and Taiwo are two case histories of endeavours, problems, and achievements in developing reading programs for newly created school systems (within the framework of burgeoning school systems). In Korea, the shift to one common language, after thirty-five years in which its use in schools was prohibited, seems to have created no problems. On the contrary, in recent years, virtually the entire school aged population achieves so-called literacy. As in many of the preceding chapters, the consistent symbol sound correspondence of an alphabet with only 24 principal symbols is cited as the chief factor in facilitating the initial stages of reading acquisition. At present, efforts associated with developing higher level reading skills have become the main area of concern.

In Nigeria, with its many national groups and languages, great efforts are directed toward developing vernacular reading programs in the main languages. At present, many children still start reading in English—a language they do not speak. Others transfer to English as the medium of instruction relatively early in their school careers. The present chapter and Abiri's recent description (1) provide an insight into conditions, forces at work, directions of developments, obstacles, and achievements to date.

Reference

1. Abiri, J.O.O. "Reading in Nigeria," *Reading Teacher*, *30* (February 1977), 509-514.

Reading and Reading Instruction in Korea: Past and Present

Byongwon Kim
Korean Institute for Research
in the Behavioral Sciences
Seoul, Korea

The Korean alphabet system, which is commonly called the *Hangul* script, was invented about 530 years ago but the equality education in reading began to succeed only recently compared to the long history of the script. Then within a rather short span of thirteen years, Korea witnessed the radical drop of 74.1 percent illiteracy rate since 1945 when she was liberated from the Japanese rule. The average level of students' comprehension, on the other hand, is estimated rather low and it is admitted that reading fails to fully play its functional role in general education. Background and probable causes will be searched in the following discussion, in the hope that readers will find it interesting and helpful in weighing and considering the basic theory of constructing an interdisciplinary reading curriculum which the author suggests at the concluding part of the paper.

To prevent you from "being lost in the chasms which result from the splitting of definitional hairs" (*13*), let me make clear the definition of reading employed in this paper. The author agrees on the operational definition of reading behavior and the tentatively summarized definition of reading produced by Gephart (*4*) and his research group which reads:

> Reading behaviors are covert responses to verbal written language. These covert responses are indicated by overperformance which could not have occurred without the responses to the written language.

Reading is a term used to refer to an interaction by which *meaning* encoded in visual stimuli by an author becomes meaning in the mind of a reader. The interaction always includes three facets: material to be read; knowledge possessed by the reader; and physiological and intellectual activities.

Note: This definition does not imply that *the* meaning intended by the author automatically becomes the readers' meaning.

Because they are or were dominant in Korea, two extremely different concepts of reading appear in this paper; namely, "responding orally to printed symbols" in the discussion of literacy and "resulting in a changed view of life which produces corresponding changes in behavior" in the discussion of functional literacy. Reading instruction or guidance has aimed at either or both of them. The author understands the former definition as that of reading at the initial stage and the latter as end-products of reading, as viewed by Clymer (*2*).

RAPID ERADICATION OF ILLITERACY

The equality education in reading began to be positively practiced by the government in 1945 when the illiteracy rate read as high as 78 percent, but the governmental survey (*3*) conducted in 1958 discloses that only 4.1 percent of those above twelve years of age are illiterate. And in 1973, only 0.8 percent of the sixth graders (twelve-year-olds) in the primary schools were reported to be illiterate in the Report on Assessing the Progress of School Education submitted by the Korean Institute for Research in the Behavioral Sciences (*10*). Compulsory education, which began to be provided in 1962, has been so successful that the rate of school enrollment of children who are school age has steadily increased to over 97 percent since 1974. The problem of equality education in reading at the initial stage is now almost completely solved, and that within this short period.

The rapid eradication of illiteracy was not accomplished because of certain miraculous teaching methods or amazingly splendid textbooks for teaching and learning Korean script. Reading has been taught in the various methods such as *spelling, word,* or *sentence.* These methods, however, often have been attacked by the proponents of the *systematic alphabet-centered* or *rote-memory of the basic syllable* methods. The *story* method was introduced in new textbooks in 1947 but no definite proof was produced that it exercised major influence upon speed in eliminating illiteracy. There has been only one textbook which has been revised or modified principally according to the curriculum changes which have taken place three times since 1945.

But the rapid mass literacy was possible under the strong leadership of the government principally because of the following facts. The Korean peninsula has been inhibited by a Mongoloid people—a single ethnic group with a common language and culture since her earliest migrants or invaders from northern China came to settle down, probably by the third millennium B.C. Even though her recorded history reveals that events on this small land have been affected by the dynamics of foreign powers (such as dynastic changes in China and the Mongolian, Japanese, and Manchu invasions), her people have fostered one culture. The Korean language which is generally considered not to be related definitely to any particular language family, is spoken exclusively in Korea. Korean is characterized by a richly developed set of derivative and conjugational affixes, which agglutinate one after another.

In addition, the Hangul or Korean alphabetic script which was developed at the instigation of King Se-jong in 1443, is a phonetic alphabet. It is a consonant-vowel script containing 24 principal symbols with 14 consonant and 10 vowel symbols and is simple and easy enough to be learned by anyone within a very short time. The Hangul alphabet is very consistent in its representation of sounds; each of the basic signs symbolizes its articulation and each syllable is written separately with the consistent pattern of consonant plus vowel, or consonant plus vowel plus consonant. That makes it easier to learn.

What, then, had occurred in Korea before 1945 concerning literacy and equality education in reading?

TOWARD EQUALITY EDUCATION IN READING

Earlier than 1443, the Hanmun or Chinese ideographic script was read by and taught to upper class males at small private elementary schools called the Sodang. The pupils spent hours at the Sodang learning to read and write the Chinese ideographs and memorizing selected passages chiefly from the works of Confucius. One of their major educational goals was to achieve a good performance in the periodic national examinations through which one could qualify for a government position.

For the middle and lower class people, the Idu system—a method of utilizing Chinese ideographs for their Koreanization—was gradually developed over a period of many centuries. In the Idu system there were four principal ways of using the Chinese ideographs (5). First, the Chinese characters were to be used with their original meanings and analogous pronunciations. Most of the Sino-Korean words or loan words from Chinese sources have originated from this category. The Sino-Korean words are thought by some authorities to represent approximately 54 percent of 150,000 entries of the Great Dictionary edited by the Korean Language Society in 1957. These are now an integral part of Korean vocabulary, for their pronunciation and usage have long been Koreanized. Second, Chinese ideographs were also to be used as a purely phonetic script. Third, great importance was attached to the original Chinese meaning. The final method was a mixture of the second and third methods, being used to write polysyllabic words. This complicated system of Idu was destined to be replaced by Hangul when it was invented.

Public acceptance of the new and easier Hangul script, however, was slow because the upper class continued to patronize the Chinese script and ridicule Hangul as "the women's script" fit only for persons of little education, the common class, and women.

It should not be overlooked, for a moment, that the Christian missionaries played an active role in the popularization of Hangul script and the eradication of illiteracy. They translated the Bible into Hangul and succeeded in attaching some value to literacy in order to make reading of the Bible possible.

In 1894, a compromise between Hangul and Hanmun scripts began to be accepted officially. A code of official conduct in government, known as the first Korean constitution embodying the spirit of the Reform of July 1894, was the most significant event in the modernizing of Korea and was promulgated by King Ko-jong. The code was written in three ways: in Hangul, in Hanmun, and then in the mixture of the two. It was the first official document written exclusively in Hangul in the history of Korea. At the same time, the government opened modern educational institutes. Furthermore, the teaching of Hangul was legalized, not as women's script but as the national script.

From then on until 1910, three ways of writing were common: Hangul, Hanmun, and a mixture of the two different scripts. Still, Hanmun learning was emphasized in the primary schools and teachers' schools.

Then the time came when Korean and the Hangul script were not permitted to be used and learned. From 1910, when Korea was subjected by the Japanese colonial administration to cultural as well as political oppression, the Japanese made a concerted effort to educate the Koreans in the Japanese language and encouraged its use. Then the Koreans were forced to accept Japanese as their national language and were prohibited from using and teaching Korean at school. Nevertheless, the Korean language was spoken among the people and the Hangul script and language were secretly taught and studied by the patriotic leaders.

The traditional, wrong attitude toward Hangul script and the Japanese rule prevented earlier achievement of equality education in reading. Today, all Korean students read books and textbooks written in Hangul only, while they are supposed to learn about 1,800 Chinese ideographs before they finish senior high school.

FUNCTIONAL LITERACY AND READING INSTRUCTION

Literacy and reading instruction discussed previously were mainly concerned about basic literacy. Now we shall look over the problems of reading and reading instruction after the initial stage. They will be weighed and considered in two phases: reading guidance and comprehension, both included in the language curriculum.

Korean students do not read many books, nor do they have high comprehension abilities. Results of survey research (6, 7, 9) recently conducted disclose that students read an average of one or two books a month and spend one or two hours a day in reading—primary and secondary school pupils and university students alike. Average scores on comprehension tests for each grade of primary and junior high schools range from the 50s to 60s (10, 12). These facts indicate that their functional reading is not developed enough to serve them as an effective and efficient tool in their life.

Since 1945, reading instruction has been thought of in two different concepts: reading guidance and comprehension teaching. Reading guidance is a systemized movement for promoting more reading of books and writing of book reports in each class under the leadership of the principal and language teachers. Reading guidance usually includes selecting books, organizing the movement, and helping students go ahead with reading books. Comprehension constitutes the most important part of language instruction throughout the educational systems. Normally, more than two-thirds of the test items constructed according to the educational and behavioral objectives cover comprehension. But neither reading guidance nor comprehension teaching is the reading instruction proper. And neither could be successful in helping the students fully develop their functional reading competence.

Reading guidance is based on the definition of reading which says that reading results in a changed view of life which produces corresponding changes in behavior. It is the end-product of reading but not the right concept of reading. Reading guidance alone could not fully aid students in developing competence for better and faster reading.

Teaching reading is one thing; teaching language and literature is another. Language and literature have their own meanings and structures, according to Phenix and Bruner (11, 1), that should be experienced by the students through their curricula organized according to the theory of discipline centered curriculum. The Korean language curriculum was revised in 1973 into a discipline-centered one. Theoretically, the role of reading in the language course has become secondary to learning the meaning and structure of linguistic and literary knowledge. Reading became a tool in learning language arts, linguistic knowledge, and literature, and it is used as a tool for learning other subjects. Now is the time to identify the role of reading and reading instruction in education. Reading should be taught in its own proper course with a systematically developed curriculum.

INTERDISCIPLINARY READING CURRICULUM

Reading as a discipline began to be introduced to Korean readers and educators early in 1974. In August, a reading research department (the first one in Korea) was established in the Korean Institute for Research in the Behavioral Sciences. The Korean Association for Reading Science, a national affiliate of the International Reading Association, was founded in 1975. About 600 research and practice reports and scholarly articles concerning reading and reading instruction were published in Korea between 1945 and 1973. At present, these are being reviewed critically in the light of further achievement of equality and quality education in begining reading and functionalization of reading competence for the eventual fulfillment of educational objectives in general.

To conclude this paper and to indicate a partial prospect of future reading and reading instruction in Korea, let me introduce an idea for the construction of an interdisciplinary reading curriculum, which I presented recently to a research meeting of the Division of Curriculum, Korean Society for the Study of Education.

My theory is that the core of functional reading competence can be described as ever-developmental power and speed of getting meaning or abstracting ideas through the process of understanding relationships of concepts represented by the visible words (8). Reading competence determines the structure and shape of the reader's covert and overt reading responses. When a reader's reading competence functions, certain influences upon his/her reading responses include reading materials, the reader's knowledge and experiences, physiological and intellectual activities, reading purposes, interest and motives, reading attitudes, and life philosophy.

On the other hand, each discipline supposedly has its own meaning and structure which are provided to the learners for their direct or vicarious experience. Theoretically, there must be an optimum reading strategy in each realm of meaning required of the learners for the maximum outcome of their learning experience. When the different reading strategies are identified, components of each strategy can be translated into behavioral objectives in the light of reading educational objectives.

The written objectives will be organized into an integrated form of spiral curriculum with the core reading competence and related facets fully considered. In addition, the content scope, sequence, and balance will also be considered together with the students' learning conditions. Reading competence consecutively developed in and through an interdisciplinary reading curriculum like this is expected to readily function in maximizing learning experiences in fields other than reading and, in turn, the learning outputs will facilitate further development of reading competence.

It is predicted that planning of an interdisciplinary reading curriculum will prove a significant one step forward in the history of reading education, to the days when school children will learn to read in the reading course proper, not "in their outside reading of stories and in their study of geography, history, and the like" (14)—also one step forward to the days when education virtually serves the new needs of individuals and our society (15) as educators help students to develop strong interests in continued study, to acquire the skills required to keep on with it, and to learn to use the intellectual apparatus of each one of the major fields of learning.

References

1. Bruner, Jerome S. *The Process of Education*. Cambridge, Massachusetts: Harvard University Press, 1960.
2. Clymer, Theodore. "What Is Reading? Some Current Concepts," in Helen M. Robinson (Ed.), *Innovation and Change in Reading Instruction*, the Sixty-seventh Yearbook of the National Society for the Study Education, Part II. Chicago: University of Chicago Press, 1968.
3. *Educational History of Korea*. Korea: Hankook Educational Research Institute, Chungang University, 1974 (in Korean).
4. Gephart, William J. *Application of the Convergence Technique to Basic Studies of the Reading Process, Final Report*. Washington, D.C.: National Center for Educational Research and Development, United States Office of Education, Project 8-0737, 149, 174, 1970.
5. Gim, Sheon-Gi. *Phonetics of Korean*. Seoul, Korea: Daehan Textbook, 1971.
6. Hwang, Kyongsook, and Kiyong Lee. "Research on the Present Situations of the Students' Reading," in *Research Review*, 12 (1976), Student Guidance Center, Ewha Womans University, Korea (in Korean).
7. Kim, Byong-Ju. "An Analytical Study on Reading Status of School Children," unpublished dissertation, Ewha Womans University, Korea, 1974 (in Korean with an English abstract).
8. Kim, Byongwon. "Core of Reading Abilities," *Readers Monthly*, 9 (August) Seoul, Korea: Samsong, 1976 (in Korean).
9. Moon, Hyung-Man, et al. "A Study on Students' Reading Improvement," *Research Review*, 7 (1975), Student Guidance Center, Chonnam National University, Korea (in Korean).
10. *National Assessment of Students Achievement Progress: Elementary and Middle School*. Korea: Korean Educational Development Institute, 1975 (in Korean).
11. Phenix, P.H. *Realms of Meaning*. New York: McGraw-Hill, 1964.
12. *Report on the Assessing of Primary School Education*. Korea: Korean Institute for Research in the Behavioral Sciences, 1973 (in Korean).
13. Staiger, Ralph C. "Reading in Today's World," in Ralph C. Staiger (Ed.), *The Teaching of Reading*. Paris: Unesco. Lexington, Massachusetts: Ginn, 1973.
14. Thorndike, Edward L. "Reading as Reasoning: A Study of Mistakes in Paragraph Reading," *Reading Research Quarterly*, 6 (Summer 1971), 425-434. Reprinted from *Journal of Educational Psychology*, 8 (June 1917).
15. Tyler, Ralph W. "What Price Quality in Education," *The Unfinished Journey: Issues in American Education*. New York: John Day, 1968.

The Problems of Beginning and Developmental Reading in Nigerian Primary Schools

Oladele Taiwo
University of Lagos
Yaba, Nigeria

INTRODUCTION

The problems of beginning and developmental reading in Nigerian primary schools derive largely from the educational system and practice in the country. The system and practice are closely related to the political structure. With nineteen state governments and a federal authority all active in the area of primary education, one should naturally expect the type of diversity of practice which we experience at present. However, with the introduction of Universal Primary Education (UPE) in September 1976, it may be possible to achieve some uniformity of practice and, perhaps, give reading the prominence it deserves on the school curriculum.

For a long time, English occupied a central position in the primary school curriculum. In many systems, English became the medium of instruction after two or three years. It was soon discovered that this led to a confused language situation in which children suffered from unsystematic teaching in both the vernacular language and English. To avoid this undesirable situation, a feeling has grown that the vernacular should be used as a medium of instruction throughout the primary school, with English being taught as a subject by a specially trained teacher. This project is usually referred to as the Vernacular Primary Project (VPP) in which at least two universities in the country have shown great interest.

With particular reference to reading, two periods of great difficulty for the children have been identified. The first period is during the first few weeks in school when children are invited to engage in activities other than those they are used to at home. Reading is one such activity. Even when started with material in the vernacular, reading as an activity is new to students and, if not properly introduced and handled, raises a number of problems for them. The second period of difficulty occurs during the transfer, after two or three years' schooling, from the vernacular to English as a medium of instruction. Conflict arises from a situation where home conditions encourage the use of the vernacular (L1) and the school sees it as its primary business to improve the children's efficiency in the use of English (L2). This situation raises problems for the children and must be taken into consideration in the development of any meaningful reading program. I felt that not enough was known about these problems in our circumstances, and I have set up a pilot research project to find out the problems of beginning and developmental reading in our primary school curriculum.

RESEARCH METHODOLOGY

My research was limited in area to thirty selected schools in Lagos State and in scope to primaries one to four of these schools. I made an intensive study of the primary school syllabus as it related to reading. Reading is not designated as a special subject in the syllabus, nor is it constituted as an area of study in its own right. But sufficient emphasis is placed on it as an important activity under the broad subject area of English, which makes it possible for a reading specialist to develop a meaningful reading program. Unfortunately, reading specialists are yet to be trained in any significant number. I discussed with teachers in the selected schools and explored with them how to improve the reading abilities of their children. I benefited especially from my interaction with teachers who had received specialist training for their work or were teaching special "English" classes.

But far more useful and reliable for the purpose of this research was the questionnaire which I sent to the schools investigated. The questionnaire was divided into two parts. Part A was devoted to acquiring some general information about the school (e.g. location, age, size, kind of school—whether church related). Information collected in Part A merely helped to throw light on the responses to the items in Part B, which was by far the more important part. In Part B, one sought to know whether a particular school had a special reading program, who was in charge of the program, and what training the person had for that position. Where there was no special reading program, questions were asked about the place of reading in the school curriculum, the problems encountered in the teaching of reading, and what the solution might be to each of these problems.

Only six out of the thirty schools had what could, by an extension of meaning, be called special reading programs. Four of them were run by teachers who had had some training for their work. All seemed limited in scope, but the teachers had no illusions about the professional disabilities under which they were working. They showed great enthusiasm and felt encouraged by the response they were getting from the pupils.

Where there were no special reading programs, adequate attention was paid to reading in the general English program. Some schools devoted as much as half of the time for English to reading or 40 percent of the total marks for English to the different kinds of reading. The key position of reading in the school curriculum seemed well established. It was generally appreciated that the children not only had to learn to read but also had to read to learn—that a good reading ability was a prerequisite to success in the other subject areas. Teachers were, therefore, naturally anxious that all obstacles in the way of children achieving this laudable goal should be removed.

Some of the obstacles identified include:

- Academically unhelpful home background.
- Poor relationship between home and school.
- Professional inadequacy of many of the teachers who handle reading.
- Insufficient supply of books and reliance on books of indifferent quality.
- Lack of reading centres and clinics.

RECOMMENDATIONS

1. *Home Background*

Children's home backgrounds should be such that encourages reading. There should be a reasonable supply of newspapers, magazines, periodicals, and books which the children can read and enjoy. If home life is completely devoid of intellectual activity, children are not likely to develop a keen interest in reading at an early age. Literate parents can help by developing a taste for reading. They do well to read, even if occasionally, to their children at bedtime.

2. Teachers of Reading

Teachers of reading should be adequately prepared for their work. It is not enough to be an English teacher; it is necessary to be a reading specialist. The success of a reading program, as with other language skills, depends on the preparation of the teacher and the usefulness of the instructional material. I suggest that in our situation, teachers should have the following qualities:

- Sufficiency in personal standard of English.
- An understanding of the needs of pupils throughout the course.
- An understanding of local needs of English as a communicational/instructional medium and requirements of L2.
- Ability to meld English teaching with the vernacular program.
- An understanding of the four basic skills and their interrelationships.
- Familiarity with the local primary school syllabus embodying those skills.
- Familiarity with many of the course books of the area.
- Ability to make annual, term, and weekly schemes of work and lesson plans for any class with necessary modifications, alterations, and supplementations for a particular class, irrespective of whether course books are available.
- Knowledge of the construction and use of required apparatus, games, etc. and the use of audiovisual aids.
- Ability to assess and improve lessons, alternating methods when appropriate.
- Ability to plan remedial work at class, group, and individual levels, and to realise the reasons for pupils' mistakes.
- Specialist training in the area of reading.

3. Books

Books constitute a major source of concern. They are not available in sufficient numbers; most of the books available at the beginning reading stage are either of poor quality or are culturally irrelevant. Space here permits only a summary of the main faults. There is an urgent need to remove these major defects.

- Inadequate reading readiness programs (at times called pre-reading activities).
- Defective ordering of structures, which violates the elementary linguistic principles of presenting the easier ones first.
- Use of passages to be read which are either unsuitable or presented in an unsuitable order. In most cases, the passages do not treat matters of intrinsic interest to the child and, therefore, cannot easily stimulate his interest. A worse fault occurs where little variety is provided in the selection of texts or passages.
- Books presented in a form not sufficiently attractive or colorful to attract children's attention.

Libraries have an important part to play in making books of different kinds available to children and they are now gradually fulfilling this role. There are many examples of good class, school, and public libraries throughout the country. There is a tendency to concentrate these facilities at the urban centres. The need to establish public libraries in the rural areas has been obvious for some time.

Teachers are becoming highly selective in the types of books they adopt for class use; only books which satisfy the objectives of a good reading program are chosen. They point out that, one common fault of the existing courses is that they do not sufficiently prepare the children for reading. Teachers seem particularly mindful of the importance and usefulness of a well-prepared reading readiness program. Nearly all courses in use at the moment recognize the need to prepare children formally for reading. Unfortunately, too little time is devoted to this preparation. It is unthinkable that only one or two terms would be devoted to a program which provides the foundation for success in language teaching. For the work in the first year, one has to bear in mind the important factor of the environments from which children have come to school. Many of them will be coming in contact with formal education, of any sort, for the first time. The school cannot, therefore, take anything for granted, and before starting to play its assigned role, an attempt should be made to make up for any deficiency in the home backgrounds of the children. This factor makes a reading readiness program very important in our situation. If we want this program to achieve the desired results, we should allocate to it as much time as particular situations demand.

4. *Reading for Personal Development*

The problems of beginning reading should not be allowed to have a permanently damaging effect on children's intellectual development. This is likely to be the case unless matters improve at the higher levels of education. Strenuous efforts should be made by the combined forces of homes and schools to overcome the difficulties of poor beginning readers. Poor readers at the level of the upper primary or lower secondary school are easily identified by poor performances in many of their school subjects. At this stage, reading has become an instrument for development, for mastering other school subjects. It becomes a means of achieving success in public examinations at the stage of upper secondary. At the university level, reading has become fully developmental and functional, a means of acquiring public recognition, and of achieving worldly success. This function continues after formal education has ended. The point to stress is that reading is a lifelong activity. Those who enjoy reading derive pleasure and satisfaction from it. The aim of any beginning reading program, therefore, is to lay such a strong foundation that children can benefit from it throughout their lives.

5. *Reading Program*

The aim should be to help the pupils achieve the following outlined objectives:

- Understand written instructions—textbooks, tables, charts, forms. (Intensive reading for meaning and understanding.)
- Correspondence—letters (informal, formal, and official) telegrams. (Extensive reading for meaning, gist, and scanning.)
- Information—newspapers, journals, notices, references.
- Pleasure—storybooks, verse, plays.

6. *Reading Centres and Clinics*

Reading centres should be established all over the country with programs designed to stimulate the child's interest in reading. Such centres, with highly qualified staff, will be able to detect early symptoms of reading disabilities, discover their probable causes and the appropriate action which the teacher should take in each case. Cases of visual, auditory, and physical defects, inefficient motor control, low mental ability, and emotional difficulties should be referred to the school medical officer, educational psychologist, or any special clinics set up for that purpose. In appropriate cases, reference should be made to parents in order to have more facts about the child's background and medical history. Health visitors and welfare officers should be called upon, as required, to help in the consideration of appropriate cases. Reading centres and clinics bring the greatest benefit to the child if they work in close collaboration with other appropriate agencies.

CONCLUSION

Reading is an instrument of national and international understanding. It is therefore very important that children acquire good reading abilities from the beginning and that they use these abilities appropriately for development. It is only then that functional reading becomes truly meaningful to them in later life. This laudable objective cannot be achieved if basic necessities are lacking or if reading is not regarded as an important activity in its own right. One can only hope that, as we continue to evolve a system of education in Nigeria, we shall accord to reading its proper role as an instrument of social change.

PART FIVE

Only when a careful, dispassionate review of the entire situation precedes all educational decisions is there hope that the many problems inherent in multilingual education will be solved according to the best professional expertise of the day. The closing chapter of this volume provides an example of just such a process in the context of planning the reading aspect of an intensive foreign language program in this case, English. The specific program described and directed by Olshtain was developed and tested by a team of experts over a period of several years and, today, the program is used extensively.

Like other authors in this volume, Olshtain is a native of the country for which her program was planned. Not surprisingly her great familiarity and identification with the specific difficulties confronting learners, whose own language and writing systems are entirely different from European languages and scripts, influence her decisions when she is called upon to choose between conflicting alternatives. As a result, some of the practices advocated, borne out by many years of careful classroom experimentation, are at variance with presently accepted usage. Thus, faced with the task of teaching children who are already proficient readers in their native language to read a language which lacks the consistent symbol-sound correspondences children expect as a matter of course, she sees no harm in enriching the meagre supply of possible practice words by adding so-called nonsense words, provided they conform to English spelling patterns. By thus accelerating decoding skills at the expense of meaning in the initial stage, she is able to draw upon facility in reading and writing in more intensive work on language acquisition and reading for meaning.

It has to be reemphasized that the initial stage of Olshtain's program is intended for fourth or fifth graders, students who already have ample experience in reading their native language.

Teaching Reading in a Foreign Language

Elite Olshtain
Tel Aviv University
Tel Aviv, Israel

INTRODUCTION

With communication distances diminishing, the need for world languages is constantly increasing. Today, more than ever before, people require a foreign or second language in order to communicate with the rest of the world. Reading in the foreign language is probably one of the most widely used means of communication.

During the past few decades, English has risen rapidly as a leading world language; as a result, ESL (English as a Second Language) and EFL (English as a Foreign Language) courses seem to flourish everywhere. The terms ESL and EFL are often used to differentiate between the teaching of English as a subject area alone—EFL—as contrasted with the teaching of English as a new language, along with its use as a medium of instruction—ESL. The distinction between the two terms is important insofar as the goals of instruction are concerned but it does not represent any real conflict in language pedagogy.

This presentation concerns itself with the teaching of reading in a foreign language in general, with specific reference to English. The ideas and procedures suggested here are largely based on the experience gained while preparing teaching materials within the Israeli school system. These materials were created to provide speakers of Hebrew and Arabic with a suitable course of study. For the Israeli learner, English is a vital and indispensable means of communication with the rest of the world; reading comprehension, perhaps, more than any other language skill, is a highly valued goal. It is the objective of this presentation to suggest some ways and means toward attaining reading competency within the EFL course of study. In order to do so, it seems profitable to view the reading course as comprising three consecutive stages, each with its specific goals: initial, intermediate, and advanced.

THE INITIAL STAGE

A competent reader is one who has, among other things, mastered the mechanics of reading and, therefore, effectively uses letter and word discrimination. The preliminary requirement of the early stage, therefore, is the mastery of the mechanics of reading in the FL. A considerable section of the course of study can be designed to help the learners gradually develop, and finally achieve, mastery of the mechanics of reading.

Since the learner at the early stage has a rather limited command of the new language, it is useful to view the reading and the language sections at the initial stage, as two separate and yet parallel parts. While the language section concerns itself with grammatical structures, the reading section focuses on the promotion and the achievement of the mastery of the mechanics of reading. Gradually, however, as the learner's mastery of the mechanics increases, the reading skill is utilized for the general use of language and the learner moves on to an intermediate stage where the four language skills (listening, speaking, reading, and writing) are combined.

Careful sequencing and structuring of the reading material at the initial stage, can greatly enhance the reading courses as a whole. This can provide the learner with the power to arrive at generalizations which will become useful stepping stones at a later stage, when more complex spelling rules are introduced.

The guiding principles of sequencing and structuring the reading material at the initial stage, relate directly to the nature of the target language and its orthography. Since we are concerned with English as a target language, we are dealing with a rather nonconsistent system of grapheme-phoneme correlation. Accordingly, the reading course contains a larger number of units than would be necessary for a more consistent system (6).

(German, for instance, can be considered as having a consistent system of a one to one grapheme-sound correlation.) The sequence and content of the units in an English reading course, can be best centered around "spelling patterns" (*8*) rather than around a one to one set of grapheme-phoneme correlations. A spelling pattern is based on two factors: the individual grapheme and its immediate environment. Thus, for instance, the vowel letter *a* will be paired with several typical environments: CVC as in *mat, cat, map*; CVCe as in *mate, hate, cape*; __r (in front of the letter *R*) as in *car, far, arm*. Each environment presents a separate unit of work, and each such unit is devoted to mastering the particular spelling pattern.

The sequencing and structuring of the units at the initial stage do not necessarily differ between the mother and the foreign language courses. In the case of English, for instance, the same basic spelling pattern constitutes the core of the course. There are, however, several other significant differences between the learners in a ML reading course and those in a FL course. Children learning to read in their native language do not know how to read but do know their language. Foreign learners, on the other hand, have a very limited knowledge of the target language, although they may be quite competent in reading in their native language. While first graders can enjoy an endless number of rhymes, limericks, and other fun activities concerned with a particular spelling pattern, foreigners are limited by the meaningful material they can handle in the new language. Some of the reading activities in the FL must, therefore, lack in meaning and concentrate on pure mechanics. Each lesson can concentrate only on a small number of meaningful key words in order to demonstrate the spelling pattern. All other practice items will have to remain nonsense words. Yet, the letter combinations in such words must be plausible in English, even when these are not real words. Thus, learners will be given the chance to develop an awareness of typical letter sequences in English.

The learners at the initial stage are often youngsters. In order to enhance their learning of the mechanics of reading, considerable practice and manipulative activities might be necessary. Reading games designed for this purpose (*1*) are often of great help in the learning process. They allow learners to develop their own strategies for the development of reading competence.

The recognition of spelling patterns, however, is not the only task that FL learners are undertaking at the early stage. If, for instance, the Roman alphabet is new to the learners, as is the case with speakers of Hebrew and Arabic, considerable time must be devoted to letter discrimination. Moreover, learners often come from a consistent grapheme-phoneme correlation system in their native language and, therefore, find the English system even harder. There are, however, a number of additional aspects of the early reading stage that have to be included in the course as accompanying features of the mechanics of reading: word discrimination, sentence recognition, proper eye movement (Hebrew and Arabic are written from right to left), and silent reading. All these subskills must be combined with the learning of the spelling patterns in order to lend an effective initial course in reading. Let us illustrate an attempt to implement the above described considerations in a first prereader text used in Israel—*English for Speakers of Hebrew 2*. The particular unit of work selected here as a sample, deals with the vowel letter *a* in the environment CVC. The key words in this lesson—namely, the meaningful words which the learner can actually use in English—are: *hat, map, pan, man.* (All the consonants have been taught earlier.) The key words are introduced orally first, within familiar language structures and accompanied by pictures or real objects.:

> This is a pan.
> The pan is big.
> The pan is here.

During the oral preparation, learners "get to know" the key words actively, within the language boundaries of their knowledge of the FL. Following the oral introduction, the key words now constitute the core of the reading lesson. The following is the first page in the prereader lesson mentioned previously.

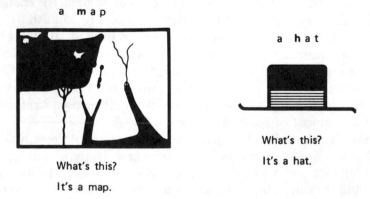

a m a p

What's this?
It's a map.

a h a t

What's this?
It's a hat.

a p a n

S a m

This is a pan.   This is Sam.

The pan is here.   Sam is a man.

The first step in the reading lesson is meaningful, "global" reading, in the sense that learners encounter "whole words" within sentences. However, the focus is on words which follow the spelling pattern. The sentences might also contain structure words which learners, at this point, read "globally" only, like the word *this*, for instance. The key words, however, guide them to the spelling pattern.

Since the objective is to help learners master the spelling pattern presented in the lesson, the key words cannot suffice. A variety of additional items is needed in order to allow the learners to practice the spelling pattern with various letter combinations.

The following is the second page in the above prereader lesson:

a	b	c	d
pat	pab	pan	pant
nat	nab	nan	band
bat	bab	ban	sand

As far as the learner is concerned, all of the above words are meaningless (even those that are not nonsense but real words). On the other hand, they all present plausible English letter sequences and, therefore, prepare the learner for proper generalizations concerning English. Other combinations like "st..." or "sp.." can be introduced at this stage as well, but care has to be taken that the learner never comes across "sr..." or "sb..." which are not English sequences.

Following the described reading practice, the lesson moves on to letter discrimination. Each learner is involved in practice of a silent and individual nature. Writing is part of the letter discrimination practice and, at this stage, one can view writing as additional reinforcement to reading.

As the lesson proceeds, meaningful reading should again replace the more mechanical procedures in which the learners were involved. We expect the learners not to be quite familiar with the spelling pattern and the individual letters that appear in the key words. These are presented again within meaningful sentences, which suit the learners' levels of knowledge in the FL. When possible, these meaningful sentences should create a little story, a joke, or some other element of interest. They could even accompany a set of comic pictures. This will give learners a feeling of achievement and progress, and motivate their interest in future reading lessons.

The initial stage of the reading course reaches its end when the four language skills can be combined. Learners then have the chance to be introduced to new language material orally, as well as through the written page. From this point on, the emphasis on the reading part of the course has to be shifted toward "reading for comprehension." The intermediate stage of the course is concerned with developing proper reading for comprehension habits.

THE INTERMEDIATE STAGE

The intermediate stage begins at the point where learners have mastered the mechanics of reading. The time has now come to distinguish between two types of reading activities: intensive reading and extensive reading. The first is usually caried out in class under the teacher's constant guidance, while the latter is done by the learners on their own.

INTENSIVE READING

The part of the course devoted to intensive reading aims at fostering good reading habits. The goal is to develop competent readers in the FL. In order to progress toward this goal, FL learners will need to expand their vocabulary stock, as well as develop effective techniques in reading comprehension. The text designed for this purpose, therefore, has a twofold function: to help learners increase their vocabulary stock and train them in reading comprehension.

The first requirement in the preparation of a suitable intensive reading text is interesting, yet simplified, reading material. By simplifying original texts, one often ends up with a diluted, watered down story which has lost its interesting aspects. Therefore, simplification and adpatation are very crucial processes. On the other hand, using material that is too hard for the learners in question, is defeating rather than achieving the goal.

How can the intensive reading program help learners develop better reading habits? Even if we assume that FL learners possess good reading habits in their native language, they now will have to adjust the habits to the new language. If students have learned to utilize various cues, redundancies, and syntactic structures in the mother tongue in order to ease the process of comprehension, they now have to learn all these in the new language. Moreover, in order to become a competent reader in the FL, the learners may have to overcome a psychological difficulty; the fact that, often, many individual words will not be familiar to them. Yet, they will be guided to try and grasp the sentence or the passage as a whole. The FL learners have to be lead to the understanding that when they know how to make use of the context and the other cues available, it is not necessary to "know" every single word in order to read and understand. Special activities should help learners become "good guessers" while reading and, subsequently, more effective readers.

Although we may assume that most students have learned to read for a purpose in their native language, retraining is now needed in the FL. It is again necessary to train learners to read for the general idea or to read for detailed information, depending on the overall purpose of their reading. In the FL too, learners must be trained to scan materials from which they want to select only relevant sections or read very quickly something which is a news item or, in some cases, read very thoroughly when they need to rely on the accurate information given in the article or chapter. All these reading skills, therefore, must be taken up again by the FL intensive reading course, although they were dealt with in the ML.

Let us consider some of the ways in which FL learners can be trained in the previously mentioned skills, within the intensive reading program. In terms of methodological procedure, we shall assume that every intensive reading selection will be read three times. In preparation for the first reading of a new text, it is important to encourage learners to read for the main idea. No matter how many individual words learners don't know, the golden rule is "try to get the main idea of the passage." In order to facilitate this process, the teacher may prepare key words and expressions to help learners through the first reading.

There are certain basic strategies which learners or beginning readers should develop in order to become more efficient readers. One such strategy is to focus on key words and ignore less important words. Syntactic function and form will help readers identify key words. Let us assume, for instance, that the following sentence appears in the text: "Water came through gigantic pipes and was pumped by atomic engines."

Looking at the sentence carefully, we can easily see that *pipes* is a key word, and so are *pump* and *engines*. The word *gigantic*, on the other hand, is not vital. At the intermediate stage of the reading course, it is still the task of the teacher to help learners by familiarizing them with most of the key words in a new reading passage. On the other hand, learners should be encouraged to disregard the fact that there are words which they do not know—*gigantic*, for instance. Various teaching techniques can be employed to train learners to disregard such words. For example, one may want to show readers the sentence without the word *gigantic*: "Water came through pipes and was pumped by atomic engines." One soon realizes that *gigantic* does not make a great difference in the idea put forward in this sentence. But how does one know that *gigantic* is the less important word here? The structure of the sentence helps: at this stage, readers should have no difficulty identifying gigantic as some kind of adjective describing pipes and, therefore, *pipes* is the vital item while the meaning of gigantic can be guessed or inferred from the context.

The first reading of text should aim at the overall understanding of the passage and, therefore, learners should be encouraged to disregard words that do not seem vital for such understanding. The second reading of the passage, however, aims at more detailed understanding. Learners are now instructed to work carefully through every paragraph. First, they must understand the main idea presented in each paragraph. Next, learners should be trained to utilize the context and the structural information in order to understand the subtleties of meaning.

The following sentence appears in a story about Jules Verne in one of the readers in the *English for Speakers of Hebrew* series, intended for the intermediate stage (the fourth or fifth year of English as a Foreign Language): "You must be tired; you travel so much." At this point, learners are probably familiar with the regular meaning of the word *must*, namely, *obligation*. Yet here, the meaning of *must* is different. It is important, therefore, to train learners to infer the meaning from the context. The following sentence might help to pinpoint the meaning:

"You must be tired" (line _____) means
a. I am sure that you are tired.
b. You are tired!
c. I suppose you are tired.
d. I don't think that you are tired but you should be.

While trying to find the most suitable answer, learners are forced into a situation of trying to use the context in order to understand the specific meaning in this case. In the correction of such a sentence, learners should be shown how one infers the right meaning from the context provided in the original sentence. "You must be tired" is obviously a conclusion drawn from the fact that "You travel so much." It is, therefore, not a fact in itself but a deduction of some sort and thus item c, "I suppose you are tired" is the closest in meaning.

Activities and exercises like the one demonstrated above train the learner in finding the meaning in the context given. One learns to utilize various strategies to promote one's understanding. The following is one paragraph from a reading passage included in the self-teaching reading course used for Everyman's English—Open University in Israel:

Line 17 "Since my return to Manchester, the weather has got worse and worse and it has been raining all the time. I need the umbrella very much, so kindly send it to me as
20 quickly as possible, by air. Naturally, the cost of sending it will be at my expense. I am sorry to cause you this trouble, but that umbrella was my favorite one."

The second reading of this passage is followed by activities such as the following:

22 ... you this trouble, but that umbrella was my favorite one.

a. The word *trouble* in line 22 means _____ .
   difficulty
   punishment
   expense
   insult
b. Which word in lines 17-22 means *price*?
c. Which word in this paragraph means *which I like best*?
d. The word *one* in line 22 refers to _____ .

These activities show how one can guide learners in utilizing the context and get deeper understanding of the paragraph. There are, of course, numerous ways of working on each paragraph in detail, and the examples show only some of these.

Finally, the third reading is intended to put all the pieces together and provide learners with a thorough understanding of the whole passage. This third reading should be followed by activities that require inference and further expansion of the content. Discussion questions and guided writing activities are suitable for this stage.

The question now arises as to how much the learners have really gained from the intensive reading activities described. The only way to evaluate that would be to present them with a previously unseen passage, which they are guided to read on their own. This passage must be carefully prepared so as to contain only key words from the learners' active vocabulary stock and other words which can be easily understood from the context. If the learners manage to cope with such "unseen" material, they have definitely improved and gained better reading habits.

EXTENSIVE READING

Learners who participate in an effective, intensive reading course will gradually be prepared for extensive reading. The latter is reading done by learners on their own, outside the classroom. At the intermediate stage of the FL course, however, even the extensive reading must initially be guided by the teacher.

Extensive reading should aim at the following objectives:

1. Help learners develop satisfaction from reading on their own.
2. Expose learners to a variety of language structures used in a natural manner.
3. Improve and promote effective reading habits.

In order to achieve these objectives, the reading material must be suited for extensive use. The first and most important requirement is interest. If we expect learners to enjoy reading, they must find the material interesting. It must be suited for the particular age group and it must be varied enough to cater to a variety of tastes: fiction, science fiction, adventure, mystery, nonfiction, biography, invention, and discovery.

The second requirement is for the material to be easy enough to be read extensively. The text should be written in simple English and yet kept natural and fluent. In order to prepare such materials, care must be taken to provide ample information about the lexical items within the context of the passage. For instance, if *rope* appears in a passage in the sentence, "He came out with a package and some rope," there is actually no way for readers to know what the meaning of *rope* is unless the sentence is followed by a second sentence such as, "He tied the package to his bicycle with the rope." Now, there is a good chance that readers will be able to guess the meaning of *rope* if they did not know this word before. It is important, therefore, to write the extensive reading materials so that readers are constantly helped in guessing from context and in utilizing the information given in order to understand better, rather than having to turn to the dictionary for every unfamiliar word. Turning to the dictionary too often makes reading a tedious job and interferes with enjoyment.

Another useful way of helping intermediate level pupils read material containing unfamiliar words, is to explain items through pictures and captions. If a passage contains the word *grab*, in a sentence like "He grabbed the boy's arm," a picture and a caption can easily explain the meaning of the word. Thus, it is possible to prepare extensive reading material which is both easy to understand and enjoyable to read. (See "Sunshine Books" listed under Textbooks at end of this chapter.)

In conclusion, the intermediate stage should combine effectively an intensive with an extensive reading program. By using the intensive course to prepare pupils for extensive reading, and by using the extensive reading in order to develop a feeling of pleasure and enjoyment in reading, we can hope to promote good and long lasting reading habits in the FL course.

The advanced stage begins at the point where the learners of the FL course of study are ready to start reading "to learn" or, in other words, read original and unsimplified materials of their own choice. At this stage, learners are expected to be effective readers who can make good use of the reading habits they have acquired at the beginner and intermediate stages. Their only limitation is a lack of experience in reading original, unadapted materials. It is, therefore, the objective of the advanced stage to help students gain experience in a variety of styles of contemporary writing.

Reading material suited for the advanced stage of the FL course of study must contain literary, semiscientific and scientific, descriptive, and journalistic types of reading selections. Thus, students will gain experience with various styles of writing and, at the same time, will become competent in reading for a specific purpose. The material must be constructed to allow students to practice reading for various purposes. Ideally, a reading text designed for the advanced level would contain selections of the four different styles mentioned previously, each with suitable activities to follow. The literary selections could be read for the overall content or story, the scientific selections for detailed information, the descriptive passages for quick scanning, and the journalistic passages for speed reading. Such a text would allow students at the advanced stage to train effectively for the various reading skills their future use of the FL will require, and will further develop the skills introduced and practiced in the intermediate stage of the course.

An integral part of the activities designed for the advanced stage will be concerned with dictionary skills and with syntactic techniques which will focus on proper understanding of complex structures in the FL. If we take English as an example, structures like relative clauses, pronominalizations, and the use of sentence connectors will have to be carefully analyzed within the context in which they appear, so that students become skilled in proper interpretation. Such activities must be dealt with at the advanced stage since, in simplified materials, such complex structures are usually avoided. In formal style they are rather common.

SUMMARY

An attempt has been made in this paper to highlight some of the specific objectives of the three major reading stages in an FL course of study. One can hardly stress enough the need to work toward clear goals at each stage, but even more important than each stage in itself, is the linkage created between the stages. In order to create an effective reading course in the FL or SL, it is crucial to design each stage both as a preparatory step for the next stage and as a follow up from the previous stage. Thus, the result is a continuum which takes learners through a complete gamut of activities, hopefully leading up to better readers in the new language.

References

1. Akavia, et al. *Play English—A Handbook for Teachers of English.* Tel Aviv, Israel: University Publishing Projects, May 1978.
2. Allen, Virginia F. "Teaching Beginning Reading: An Interview," *Form,* 15 (April 1977).
3. Been, Sheila. "Reading in the Foreign Language Teaching Program," *Tesol Quarterly,* 9 (September 1975).
4. Berman, Ruth. "Analytic Syntax: A Technique for Advanced Reading," *Tesol Quarterly,* 9 (September 1975).
5. Dubin, Fraida, and Elite Olshtain. *Facilitating Language Learning.* New York: McGraw-Hill, 1977.
6. Feitelson, Dina. "Sequence and Structure in a System with Consistent Sound Symbol Correspondence," in J. Merritt (Ed.), *New Horizons in Reading.* Newark, Delaware: International Reading Association, 1976, 269-277.
7. Feitelson, Dina. "The Relationship between Systems of Writing and the Teaching of Reading," in M. Jenkinson (Ed.), *Reading Instruction: An International Forum.* Newark, Delaware: International Reading Association, 1967, 191-199.
8. Fries, Charles C. *Linguistics and Reading.* New York: Holt, Rinehart and Winston, 1963.
9. Olshtain, Elite. "Planning a Reading Programme," *English Teachers' Journal,* 13 (April 1975), Israel.
10. Olshtain, Elite. "Implementing the Intensive Reading Program," *English Teachers' Journal,* 14 (November 1975), Israel.
11. Olshtain, Elite. "First Steps in Estensive Reading," *English Teachers' Journal,* 16 (December 1976), Israel.
12. Norris, William E. "Advanced Reading: Goals, Techniques, Procedures," *Forum,* 13 (1975).
13. Smith, Frank. *Understanding Reading.* New York: Holt, Rinehart and Winston, 1971.

Textbooks

1. *English for Speakers of Hebrew.* Constructed by the English Materials Project, Tel Aviv University, University Publishing Projects, 28 Hanatsiv Street, Tel Aviv, Israel.
2. *Everyman's English.* Everyman's University, Box 39328, Ramat Aviv, Tel Aviv, Israel.
3. "Sunshine Books," ESL/EFL Extensive Readers. University Publishing Projects, 28 Hanatsiv Street, Tel Aviv, Israel.